sea food

sea food

Kay Scarlett

LAUREL
GLEN

San Diego, California

Contents

Starters

Fried whitebait

1 lb. 2 oz. whitebait
2 teaspoons sea salt
2 tablespoons all-purpose flour
1½ tablespoons cornstarch
2 teaspoons finely chopped Italian
   parsley
vegetable oil, for deep-frying
lemon wedges, for serving

Combine the whitebait and sea salt in a bowl and mix well. Cover and refrigerate until needed.

Combine the flour, cornstarch, and parsley in a bowl and season well with freshly ground black pepper. Fill a deep-fat fryer or large saucepan one-third full of oil and heat to 350°F or until a cube of white bread dropped into the oil browns in 15 seconds. Toss a third of the whitebait in the flour mixture, shake off the excess flour, and deep-fry for 1½ minutes or until pale and crisp. Drain well on crumpled paper towels. Repeat with the remaining whitebait.

Just before serving, reheat the oil to 375°F or until a cube of white bread browns in 10 seconds, and fry the whitebait a second time, in batches, for 1 minute each batch or until lightly browned. Drain on crumpled paper towels, salt lightly (this will help absorb any excess oil), and serve while hot with some lemon wedges.

Serves 4

Grilled sardines with basil and lemon

1 lemon, cut into thin slices
8 whole sardines, gutted, scaled,
   and cleaned
coarse sea salt
1/3 cup olive oil
3 tablespoons torn basil leaves or
   whole small leaves

Fish substitution
   small herring, mackerel

Preheat a broiler or griddle to very hot. Insert a couple slices of lemon inside each sardine and season on both sides with the sea salt and some freshly ground black pepper. Drizzle them with half of the olive oil.

Put the sardines on a baking tray and broil for 3 minutes on each side or place the fish directly onto the griddle. Check to see if the fish are cooked by lifting the top side and looking at the inside of the fish. The flesh should be opaque. When cooked, remove and place in a shallow serving dish. Sprinkle the basil over the sardines and drizzle with the remaining olive oil. Serve warm or at room temperature.

Serves 4

Cuban-style shrimp with rum

¹/₂ cup white rum
a few drops of hot pepper sauce
zest and juice of 1 lime
2 teaspoons Worcestershire sauce
2¹/₂ tablespoons all-purpose flour
generous pinch of ground cumin
generous pinch of freshly grated
   nutmeg
24 tiger shrimp, peeled and
   deveined, tails intact
2 tablespoons butter
¹/₃ cup olive oil
4 large garlic cloves, crushed
1 tablespoon chopped parsley
1 tablespoon chopped cilantro

Fish substitution
   freshwater crayfish

Mix together the rum, hot pepper sauce, lime zest and juice, and Worcestershire sauce in a small bowl.

Mix the flour with the cumin and nutmeg and season with salt and freshly ground black pepper. Dip the shrimp in the seasoned flour to lightly coat before cooking.

Melt half of the butter with half of the oil in a large sauté or frying pan and, when hot, add half of the garlic and half of the shrimp. Cook for 4–5 minutes or until the shrimp have turned a pale pink color and are lightly golden on the outside. Lift onto a serving plate and keep warm. Repeat with the remaining butter, oil, garlic, and shrimp.

Pour the rum mixture into the pan and allow to bubble for 30–40 seconds, stirring. Season with salt. Mix together the parsley and cilantro. Pour the sauce over the shrimp and sprinkle with the herbs before serving.

Serves 4

Tempura with soy and ginger dipping sauce

7 oz. shelled large shrimp, peeled and
    deveined, tails intact
10½ oz. skinned haddock fillets
2 teaspoons finely grated fresh ginger
1 tablespoon mirin
½ cup soy sauce
vegetable oil, for deep-frying
2 cups tempura flour (see Note)
1 large egg, lightly beaten
1 cup plus 1 tablespoon iced water

Fish substitution
    bream, cod, rock cod, calamari,
    lobster, crayfish

Make three cuts on the underside of each shrimp and straighten them out. Cut the fish into bite-size chunks.

Mix the ginger and mirin into the soy sauce and dilute to taste with up to 2½ tablespoons of water. Pour the sauce into dipping bowls.

Fill a deep-fat fryer or large saucepan one-third full of oil and heat to 350°F or until a cube of white bread dropped into the oil turns golden brown in 15 seconds.

Put the flour in a large bowl. Whisk the egg into the iced water. Very lightly whisk the iced water and egg into the tempura flour—it should still be lumpy. (If you overwork the batter at this stage, you will not end up with a light coating.) Dip the shrimp and fish in the batter in batches and fry until crisp and golden. Drain on crumpled paper towels and serve immediately with the dipping sauce.

Serves 4

Note: Tempura flour is an especially fine flour available at Asian markets. If you can't find it, use 1½ cups all-purpose flour and ½ cup rice flour.

Oyster po'boys

½ cup self-rising flour
¼ teaspoon cayenne pepper
¼ teaspoon paprika
1 small egg
½ cup milk
vegetable oil, for deep-frying
18 oysters, shucked

Sift the flour, cayenne pepper, paprika, and a pinch of salt into a bowl. Beat the egg and milk together and gradually add to the flour, whisking to give a smooth batter.

Fill a deep-fat fryer or large saucepan one-third full of oil and heat to 350°F or until a cube of white bread dropped into the oil turns golden brown in 15 seconds. Pat dry the oysters, dip into the batter, and deep-fry in batches for 1–2 minutes or until golden brown. Drain on crumpled paper towels and serve immediately either as they are or sandwiched between crusty bread.

Makes 18

Cajun popcorn shrimp

1 egg
1 cup milk
¾ cup all-purpose flour
¼ cup fine cornmeal
½ teaspoon baking powder
1½ teaspoons Cajun spice mix
¼ teaspoon dried basil
½ teaspoon celery salt
vegetable oil, for deep-frying
2 lb. 4 oz. shrimp, peeled and
   deveined
mayonnaise, for serving

Beat the egg and milk together. Sift the flour into a large bowl, then add the cornmeal, baking powder, Cajun spice mix, basil, and celery salt. Make a well in the center, gradually add half the beaten egg mixture, and whisk until you have a smooth paste. Add the remaining egg mixture, mix well, and leave to stand for 30 minutes to rest the batter and allow the starch to expand.

Fill a deep-fat fryer or a large saucepan one-third full of oil and heat to 350°F or until a cube of white bread dropped in the oil browns in 15 seconds.

Pat dry the shrimp with paper towels. Dip the shrimp in the batter and allow any excess batter to drain off. Cook in small batches in the oil until crisp and lightly golden. Remove with a slotted spoon or strainer and drain on crumpled paper towels. Serve hot with mayonnaise or another dipping sauce of your choice.

Serves 6

Gravlax

¼ cup sugar
2 tablespoons coarse sea salt
1 teaspoon crushed black
  peppercorns
5½ lb. good-quality salmon, filleted,
  skin left on
1 tablespoon vodka or brandy
2 tablespoons very finely chopped dill
2 tablespoons chopped dill, extra

Mustard sauce
½ cup olive oil
2 tablespoons Dijon mustard
1½ tablespoons cider vinegar
2 teaspoons chopped dill
1 teaspoon superfine sugar

Combine the sugar, salt, and crushed pepper in a small dish.

Remove any bones from the salmon with tweezers or your fingers. Pat dry with paper towels and lay a fillet skin-side down in a shallow tray. Sprinkle the fish with half the vodka, rub half the sugar mixture into the flesh, then sprinkle with 2 tablespoons of the dill. Sprinkle the flesh side of the other salmon fillet with the remaining vodka and then rub the remaining sugar mixture into the flesh. Lay it flesh-side down on top of the other fillet. Cover with plastic wrap, place a heavy board on top, and weigh the board down with three heavy cans so that the salmon is being flattened. Refrigerate for 24 hours, carefully turning it over after 12 hours.

For the mustard sauce, whisk all the ingredients together.

Uncover the salmon and lay both fillets on a board. Brush off all the dill and seasoning using a stiff pastry brush. Sprinkle with the extra dill and press it onto the flesh, shaking off any excess. Serve whole or thinly sliced on an angle toward the tail, with the mustard sauce on the side.

Serves 12

Smoked salmon
and arugula salad

Dressing
2 tablespoons extra-virgin olive oil
1 tablespoon balsamic vinegar

1 bunch arugula leaves
1 avocado
9 oz. smoked salmon slices
12 oz. marinated goat cheese,
   drained and crumbled
2 tablespoons roasted hazelnuts,
   roughly chopped

Fish substitution
   smoked trout

For the dressing, thoroughly whisk together the oil and vinegar in a bowl. Season to taste.

Trim the long stems from the arugula. Rinse the leaves, pat dry, and gently toss in a bowl with the dressing.

Cut the avocado into wedges. Put about three wedges on each serving plate with the salmon and arugula. Sprinkle the cheese and nuts over the top and season with freshly ground black pepper.

Serves 4

Taramasalata

5 slices of white bread, crusts
   removed
1/3 cup milk
3 1/2 oz. tarama (gray mullet roe)
1 egg yolk
1/2 small onion, grated
1 garlic clove, crushed
2 tablespoons lemon juice
1/3 cup olive oil
white pepper, to taste
bread, for serving

Fish substitution
   smoked cod roe

Soak the bread in the milk for
10 minutes. Press in a strainer to
extract any excess milk, then mix the
bread in a food processor with the
tarama, egg yolk, onion, and garlic for
30 seconds or until smooth. Mix in
1 tablespoon of the lemon juice.

With the motor running, slowly pour
in the olive oil until the mixture is
smooth. Add the remaining lemon
juice and a pinch of white pepper. If
the dip tastes too salty, add another
piece of bread and blend it together.
Serve the dip with bread.

Makes 1 1/2 cups

Blini with caviar

1³/₄ cups hot milk
1 tablespoon dried yeast
1 cup plus a heaping ¹/₃ cup
  all-purpose flour
heaping ¹/₃ cup buckwheat flour
2 large eggs, separated
6 tablespoons butter
¹/₂ cup plus 2 tablespoons
  vegetable oil
1¹/₄ cups sour cream
7 oz. caviar

Fish substitution
  salmon roe, lumpfish roe

Pour half the milk into a bowl, sprinkle with the yeast and a tablespoon of the all-purpose flour, and whisk well. Leave for 15 minutes or until it froths.

Sift the flours and ¹/₄ teaspoon salt into a large bowl. Add the yeast mixture and the remaining milk. Mix until you have a smooth batter. Cover with a damp towel and leave in a warm place until the mixture doubles in size and bubbles, which will take between 1 and 1¹/₂ hours.

Whisk the egg whites until stiff peaks form. Stir the egg yolks into the batter, then fold in the egg whites. Cover and leave to rise for 10 minutes. Pour the mixture into a bowl.

Heat 2 tablespoons of the butter and 2 tablespoons of the oil in a large frying pan and add 1¹/₂ tablespoons batter. Cook for 30–60 seconds or until small bubbles appear in the blini and it begins to turn golden. Flip it over and cook for 1–2 minutes on the other side. Repeat with the remaining batter, adding more butter and oil as needed. Top each blini with sour cream and a little caviar.

Serves 8

Scallop seviche

16 scallops in their shells, cleaned
1 teaspoon finely grated lime zest
$1/4$ cup lime juice
2 garlic cloves, chopped
2 red chilies, deseeded and chopped
1 tablespoon chopped cilantro
1 tablespoon olive oil
cilantro leaves, for serving

Take the scallops off their shells, but don't throw away the shells.

In a nonmetallic bowl, mix together the lime zest and juice, garlic, chilies, chopped cilantro, and the olive oil and season with salt and pepper. Put the scallops in the dressing and stir to coat. Cover with plastic wrap and refrigerate for 2 hours. The acid from the lime juice will "cold-cook" the scallop meat, turning it white.

To serve, slide each scallop back onto a half-shell and spoon a little of the lime dressing over each of the scallops. Top each one with a cilantro leaf. Serve cold.

Serves 4

Thai fish cakes

1 lb. skinned firm white fish fillets,
    such as cod or hake
¼ cup rice flour
1 tablespoon fish sauce
1 egg, lightly beaten
3 tablespoons coriander
1 tablespoon red curry paste
1–2 teaspoons chopped red chilies
    (optional)
¾ cup green beans, very thinly sliced
2 scallions, finely chopped
vegetable oil, for frying
sweet chili sauce, for serving
chopped peanuts and finely diced
    cucumber (optional), for garnish

Fish substitution
    ling, redfish

Roughly chop the fish into chunks,
then process in a food processor for
20 seconds or until smooth.

Add the rice flour, fish sauce, egg,
coriander, curry paste, and chilies, if
using. Process for 10 seconds or until
well combined, then transfer to a
large bowl. Alternatively, finely chop
and blend by hand. Mix in the green
beans and scallions. With wet hands,
form 2 tablespoons of mixture at a
time into flat patties.

Heat the oil in a heavy-based frying
pan over medium heat. Cook four fish
cakes at a time until golden brown on
both sides. Drain on crumpled paper
towels, then serve with sweet chili
sauce. The sauce can be garnished
with a sprinkling of chopped peanuts
and finely diced cucumber.

Serves 4–6

Oysters with ginger and lime

12 oysters, shucked, in their shells
½ teaspoon finely grated fresh ginger
zest and juice of 2 limes
2 teaspoons Thai fish sauce
1 tablespoon chopped cilantro
2 teaspoons sugar
lime wedges, for serving

Nestle the opened oysters on a bed of crushed ice or rock salt on a large platter (this will keep them steady).

Mix the ginger, lime zest and juice, fish sauce, cilantro, and sugar together. Drizzle a little of the sauce into each oyster shell and serve with lime wedges.

Serves 2

Sardine patties

1 lb. sardines, gutted
1 thick slice of white bread, crusts
  removed
1 large garlic clove, crushed
2 tablespoons chopped parsley
pinch of ground cumin
pinch of ground paprika
2 large eggs, lightly beaten
⅓ cup all-purpose flour, plus a little
  extra for dusting
3–4 tablespoons vegetable oil
lemon wedges, for serving

Fish substitution
  herring, mackerel

Cut each sardine into two fillets and remove the flesh from the skins. Remove as many of the bones as possible using tweezers. Roughly chop the flesh and put in a bowl.

Put the bread in a food processor and whizz into fine crumbs or chop finely by hand. Add the fish, garlic, parsley, cumin, paprika, beaten eggs, and flour and process until roughly combined. Season with salt and mix. With lightly floured hands, form the mixture into six balls and place on a plate. Cover and chill in the fridge for 30 minutes before cooking.

Heat the oil in a large frying pan and, when hot, add three of the balls. Once in the pan, flatten them out slightly into patties. Cook for 4–5 minutes on each side or until golden brown and cooked through. Drain on crumpled paper towels and keep warm. Repeat with the rest of the balls, adding more oil if necessary. Serve with the lemon wedges.

Makes 6

Steamed clams with corn and bacon

2 tablespoons butter
1 large onion, chopped
6 bacon strips, chopped
3 lb. 5 oz. fresh clams, cleaned
1 large ear of corn, kernels removed
1/2 cup plus 2 tablespoons dry cider
1/2 cup plus 2 tablespoons heavy
  cream

Fish substitution
  pipis, cockles, mussels

Melt the butter in a large saucepan and, when hot, add the onion and bacon. Cook over medium heat for about 5 minutes or until the onion is soft and the bacon is cooked.

Tip the clams into a large saucepan with 1/4 cup water and place over medium–high heat. Once the water is hot and the clams begin to steam, cover with a lid and cook for 2–3 minutes or until they have opened. Drain, reserving the liquid, then strain the liquid through a fine sieve. Discard any clams that have not opened.

Add the corn kernels to the onion and bacon and cook for 3–4 minutes or until tender, stirring. Pour in the cider and 1/4 cup of the reserved clam cooking liquid. Bring to a boil, then simmer for 2 minutes. Stir in the cream and season with salt and pepper. Tip in the clams and toss them in the sauce. Serve in warm, deep bowls.

Serves 4

Jumbo shrimp with garlic, chili, and parsley

2 tablespoons butter
scant ½ cup olive oil
2 large garlic cloves, finely chopped
1 small red chili, deseeded and finely
  chopped
16 jumbo shrimp
3 tablespoons chopped Italian parsley
lemon wedges, for serving

Fish substitution
  tiger shrimp

Heat the butter and oil together in a large frying pan and, when hot, add the garlic and chili. Cook, stirring all the time, for 30 seconds. Add the shrimp and cook for 3–4 minutes on each side or until they turn pink.

Sprinkle the shrimp with the parsley and serve immediately on hot plates with the lemon wedges to squeeze over them.

Serves 4

Note: If you like, you can heat up individual iron or stoneware dishes, transfer the just-cooked shrimp to them, and serve the shrimp still sizzling. Remember to provide plenty of napkins.

Crab cakes with avocado salsa

12 oz. fresh crabmeat
2 eggs, lightly beaten
1 scallion, finely chopped
1 tablespoon mayonnaise
2 teaspoons sweet chili sauce
1 1/4 cups fresh white bread crumbs
vegetable oil, for shallow-frying
all-purpose flour, for dusting
lime wedges, for serving

Avocado salsa
2 ripe Roma tomatoes, chopped
1 small red onion, finely chopped
1 large ripe avocado, diced
1/4 cup lime juice
2 tablespoons chervil leaves
1/2 teaspoon superfine sugar

Fish substitution
canned crabmeat

Pick over the crabmeat and pull out any stray pieces of shell or cartilage. Combine the crabmeat, eggs, scallion, mayonnaise, sweet chili sauce, and bread crumbs in a bowl, season with salt and black pepper, then stir well. Using wet hands, form the crab mixture into eight small, flat patties. Cover and put in the fridge for 30 minutes.

For the avocado salsa, put the tomato, onion, avocado, lime juice, chervil leaves, and sugar in a bowl. Season to taste with salt and freshly ground black pepper and toss gently to combine.

Heat the oil in a large frying pan over medium heat. Dust the crab cakes with flour and cook for 3 minutes on each side or until golden brown—turn them only once so they don't break up. Drain on crumpled paper towels. Serve the crab cakes with the avocado salsa and lime wedges.

Serves 4

Sugarcane shrimp with dipping sauce

Shrimp mix
14 oz. shrimp, peeled and deveined
1 egg white
1 teaspoon ground coriander
2 red Asian shallots, peeled and
    roughly chopped
3 garlic cloves, peeled and
    roughly chopped
1 teaspoon brown sugar
1 teaspoon fish sauce
1 stem of lemongrass, white part only,
    cut into three pieces
1 tablespoon chopped Vietnamese
    mint or other mint leaves
1 teaspoon salt

Cucumber dipping sauce
1 tablespoon rice vinegar
1 tablespoon lime juice
1 tablespoon fish sauce
¼ teaspoon sambal oelek (see Notes)
1 teaspoon sugar
1 tablespoon finely chopped,
    peeled cucumber

15 (4-inch) lengths of thin sugarcane
    (approximately ½ inch diameter),
    peeled (see Notes)
vegetable oil, for deep-frying

Put the shrimp in a food processor with half the egg white and all of the remaining ingredients for the shrimp mix. Process to a paste. Alternatively, chop finely and mix by hand. Add just enough of the remaining egg white to bind the mixture. Pour the mixture out onto a large plate. Cover and chill for 30 minutes in the fridge.

Mix all the ingredients for the dipping sauce together in a small bowl.

Put a tablespoon of the shrimp mixture in the palm of your hand. Press the end of a piece of sugarcane into the middle of the mixture, then firmly mold the mixture in your palm around the cane so that it covers about 2½ inches of the cane. Transfer to a board and repeat with the remaining shrimp mixture and pieces of sugarcane so that you have fifteen sugarcane shrimp in total.

Fill a deep-fat fryer or large saucepan one-third full of oil. Heat the oil to 350°F or until a small cube of white bread dropped into the oil turns golden brown in 15 seconds.

Cook three shrimp sticks at a time for 4–5 minutes or until the shrimp mixture turns a light golden brown. Turn halfway through cooking to ensure they brown evenly. Remove from the oil using tongs and drain on paper towels. Cool for a few minutes before serving. Serve with the bowl of dipping sauce.

Makes 15

Notes: Sambal oelek is a hot paste made from fresh red chilies and other seasonings. It can be found in the Asian foods section of many supermarkets and it will keep for months if stored in the refrigerator.

It is nearly impossible to find fresh pieces of sugarcane. Packaged sugarcane is sold in some speciality stores; it has been boiled before being packaged to make it edible. Peel away the brownish skin from the white flesh before using.

Clams in yellow bean sauce

1 tablespoon vegetable oil
2 garlic cloves, crushed
1 tablespoon grated fresh ginger
2 tablespoons yellow bean sauce
   (see Note)
3 lb. 5 oz. hard-shelled clams,
   cleaned
½ cup chicken stock
white pepper, to taste
1 scallion, finely chopped

Fish substitution
   any type of clam

Heat a wok until very hot, add the oil, and heat until hot. Stir-fry the garlic and ginger for 30 seconds, then add the yellow bean sauce and clams and toss together. Add the chicken stock and stir until the clams have all opened, discarding any that do not open after 3 minutes. Season with salt and white pepper. Transfer the clams to a bowl or plate and sprinkle with the scallion.

Serves 4

Note: Yellow bean sauce is sometimes sold as fermented yellow soybean paste. It can be found in the Asian foods section of some supermarkets. If yellow bean sauce is unavailable, use the similarly flavored brown bean sauce or the stronger-flavored black bean sauce.

Salmon carpaccio

1 lb. 2 oz. sashimi-grade piece
  of salmon
3 vine-ripened tomatoes
1 tablespoon baby capers, rinsed
  and squeezed dry
1 tablespoon chopped dill
1 tablespoon extra-virgin olive oil
1 tablespoon lime juice
crusty bread, for serving

Fish substitution
  fresh tuna, smoked salmon

Wrap the salmon in foil and freeze for 20–30 minutes or until partly frozen.

Meanwhile, score a cross in the base of each tomato, put in a bowl, and cover with boiling water. Let stand for 30 seconds, then plunge the tomatoes into cold water and peel the skin away from the cross. Cut each tomato in half, scoop out the seeds with a spoon, and dice the flesh. Put the flesh in a bowl and stir in the capers and dill.

Remove the salmon from the freezer and unwrap. Using a very sharp knife, carefully cut the salmon into thin slices across the grain. Cover four serving plates with the slices in a thin layer. Alternatively, you can serve the salmon on a platter.

Whisk together the olive oil and lime juice in a small bowl and season with a large pinch of salt or sea salt. Drizzle this dressing over the salmon just before serving. Season with pepper and serve immediately with the tomato mixture and bread.

Serves 4

Tandoori-style shrimp

³/₄ teaspoon saffron threads
1 small onion, quartered
3 garlic cloves, peeled
2 teaspoons grated fresh ginger
2 tablespoons lemon juice
½ teaspoon chili powder
1 teaspoon paprika
pinch of ground coriander
pinch of ground cumin
2 teaspoons garam masala
1–2 drops red food coloring (optional)
1 tablespoon vegetable oil
scant 1 cup yogurt
30 shrimp, peeled and deveined,
   tails intact
lemon wedges and naan bread,
   for serving

Fish substitution

chunks of sea bream, cod, sea bass

Soak the saffron in 1 tablespoon hot water for 5 minutes. Add the saffron and its soaking liquid to a food processor with the onion, garlic, ginger, lemon juice, chili powder, paprika, coriander, cumin, garam masala, food coloring (if using), oil, and 1 teaspoon salt. Process to a paste. Scoop into a bowl and stir in the yogurt.

Thread five shrimp onto each of six metal skewers (if you're using bamboo skewers, soak them in water for 30 minutes first). Put in a nonmetallic, ovenproof dish (pick one that will fit in your oven) and cover with the marinade. Cover with plastic wrap and refrigerate for 2–3 hours. Allow the shrimp to come to room temperature. Preheat the oven to 450°F. Remove the plastic wrap from the dish, then bake the shrimp in the dish for 5–10 minutes or until cooked.

Remove the skewers from the marinade (they will be very hot) and put on a foil-lined baking tray. Cook under a hot broiler for 2 minutes on each side or until lightly browned and the marinade has dried up. Serve with lemon wedges and naan bread.

Serves 6

Seafood terrine

14 oz. skinned pike fillet, cut into
  bite-size pieces and well chilled
2 large egg whites
scant 1 cup heavy cream
1 tablespoon lemon juice
1 tablespoon chopped dill
1 teaspoon chopped chives
pinch of freshly grated nutmeg
white pepper, to taste
4 oz. skinned salmon fillet cut into
  short, thin strips

Fish substitution
  cod or carp (instead of the pike),
  trout (instead of the salmon)

Line a loaf pan (8 x 4 x 2¹/₂ inches)
with baking parchment and lightly
oil the parchment. Using a food
processor, blend the pike to a smooth
paste. Add the egg whites, cream,
lemon juice, dill, and chives and
process briefly using the pulse button.
Season with nutmeg, salt, and white
pepper.

Preheat the oven to 350°F. Transfer
half of the pike mixture to the loaf
pan. Lay the salmon strips on top, all
facing the same direction crosswise
so the terrine will cut easily. Season
with salt and white pepper and cover
with the remaining pike mixture.
Cover with foil and place in a roasting
pan. Add boiling water to the roasting
pan until one-third of the loaf pan is
immersed in water.

Bake for 40–45 minutes or until firm
to the touch. Remove the pan from
the water and leave until cold. Chill
overnight in the fridge. Lay a large
plate over the top of the pan and
invert it so that the terrine comes out
onto the plate. Peel off the parchment
and serve in slices. Great with a
watercress and cucumber salad.

Serves 6

Moules marinières

3½ tablespoons butter
1 large onion, chopped
½ celery stalk, chopped
2 garlic cloves, crushed
1¾ cups white wine
1 bay leaf
2 thyme sprigs
4½ lb. mussels, cleaned
scant 1 cup heavy cream
2 tablespoons chopped parsley
bread, for serving

Melt the butter in a large saucepan over medium heat. Add the onion, celery, and garlic and cook, stirring occasionally, for about 5 minutes or until the onion is softened but not browned.

Add the wine, bay leaf, and thyme to the saucepan and bring to a boil. Add the mussels, cover the pan tightly, and simmer over low heat for 2–3 minutes, shaking the pan occasionally. Use tongs to lift out the mussels as they open and put them into a warm dish. Throw away any mussels that haven't opened after 3 minutes.

Strain the liquid through a fine sieve lined with muslin into a clean saucepan to get rid of any grit or sand. Bring to a boil and boil for 2 minutes. Add the cream and simmer. Season well. Serve the mussels in individual bowls with the liquid poured over them. Sprinkle with the parsley and serve with plenty of bread.

Serves 6

Spicy fish cakes

2 small dried red chilies, stalks
  removed
14 pieces of banana leaf measuring
  6½ x 5 inches (see Note)
1 lb. grouper fillets, skinned and cut
  into chunks
1 stem of lemongrass, cut into three
  pieces
1 small onion, cut in half
1 large garlic clove, peeled
generous pinch of ground turmeric
1 teaspoon brown sugar
1 teaspoon ground coriander
1 teaspoon shrimp paste
1 tablespoon candlenuts or unsalted
  macadamias or peanuts
1 tablespoon chopped mint
1 tablespoon chopped cilantro
¼ cup coconut milk

Fish substitution
  hapuka, blue warehou, halibut,
  haddock, snapper

Soak the chilies in boiling water. Soak
fourteen cocktail sticks in cold water.
If you are using fresh banana leaves,
blanch them in boiling water for a
minute, then drain and rinse in cold
water.

Put the fish in a food processor and
blend to a thick puree. Scoop into a
bowl. Drain the chilies and put in
the processor along with the rest of
the ingredients and a pinch of salt.
Blend to a paste. Add the paste to
the fish and mix well.

Drain the cocktail sticks. Put about
2 tablespoons of mixture in the middle
of each piece of banana leaf. Fold the
shorter sides of the rectangle into the
middle so they overlap. Tuck the two
protruding ends underneath to make
a small parcel. Secure the two ends
with a cocktail stick. Put the parcels
smooth-side down on a flat barbecue
plate or heated frying pan and cook
for 5 minutes or until the banana leaf
has lightly browned and the parcels
are hot in the middle. Unwrap before
eating.

Makes 14

Note: You can buy banana leaves
from Asian markets, or you can use
foil instead.

Drunken shrimp

24 large shrimp, peeled and deveined
$^1/_2$ cup plus 2 tablespoons Chinese
  rice wine (see Note)
2 red chilies, thinly sliced
1 teaspoon finely grated fresh ginger
2 teaspoons sugar

Put the shrimp in a nonmetallic bowl.
Mix the rice wine with the chilies,
ginger, and sugar and pour over
the shrimp. Leave to marinate for
30 minutes.

Heat a wok until very hot. Take
$^1/_4$ cup of the rice wine out of the
marinade and add to the wok.
Heat it until it is very hot, then very
carefully light it either with a match
or by tipping the side of the wok
toward the gas flame. Let the flame
burn and die down before adding
the rest of the marinade and shrimp.
Cook for 2–3 minutes or until the
shrimp turn pink. Serve immediately.

Serves 4

Note: Chinese rice wine is a
fermented rice wine with a rich,
sweetish taste, similar to dry sherry.
It is sometimes called Shaoxing
rice wine.

Stir-fried crabs with tamarind sauce

2 large or 4 small live mud crabs
1/4 cup vegetable oil
2 large garlic cloves, crushed
2 small red chilies, deseeded and
  finely chopped

Tamarind sauce
1/4 cup sweet chili sauce
1 tablespoon Thai fish sauce
2 tablespoons soy sauce
2 tablespoons tamarind puree or
  lemon juice
2 tablespoons brown sugar
1 cup coconut milk
1 tablespoon water

Fish substitution
  any other type of crab

Freeze the crabs for 1 hour to immobilize them. Plunge them into boiling water for 2 minutes, then drain. Wash well with a stiff brush, then pat dry. Pull the apron back from underneath the crab and separate the shells. Remove the feathery gills and intestines. Twist off the claws. Using a cleaver or large knife, cut the crabs in half. Crack the claws using crab crackers or the back of a heavy knife.

Heat 2 tablespoons of the oil in a wok until just beginning to smoke. Carefully add half of the crab pieces. Stir for 1 minute, reduce the heat to medium, and cover with a lid. Cook for 5–7 minutes or until the crab shells turn bright red. Lift onto a plate, then repeat with the rest of the crab.

Mix together the ingredients for the tamarind sauce in a bowl. Add the last of the oil to the wok and, when hot, add the garlic and chilies. Cook for a minute, stirring, then add the sauce mixture. Bring to a boil, then reduce the heat to medium and leave to simmer, without a lid, for 8–10 minutes or until you have a thick sauce. Return the crab to the wok and stir to coat in the sauce. Remove to a serving plate and spoon the sauce over the top.

Serves 4

Salt-and-pepper calamari

2 lb. 4 oz. calamari tubes, halved
  lengthwise
1 cup lemon juice
2 cups cornstarch
1½ tablespoons salt
1 tablespoon ground white pepper
2 teaspoons superfine sugar
4 egg whites, lightly beaten
vegetable oil, for deep-frying
lemon wedges, for serving
cilantro, for garnish

Open out the calamari tubes, wash, and pat dry. Lay on a chopping board with the insides facing up. Score a fine diamond pattern on the calamari, being careful not to cut all the way through. Cut into pieces of about 2 x 1¼ inches. Place in a flat, nonmetallic dish and pour the lemon juice on top. Cover and refrigerate for 15 minutes. Drain and pat dry.

Combine the cornstarch, salt, white pepper, and sugar in a bowl. Dip the calamari into the egg white and then into the flour mixture, shaking off any excess.

Fill a deep-fat fryer or large saucepan one-third full of oil and heat to 350°F or until a small cube of white bread dropped into the oil turns golden brown in 15 seconds. Cook batches of the calamari for 1–2 minutes or until the flesh turns white and curls. Drain on crumpled paper towels. Serve with lemon wedges and garnish with cilantro.

Serves 6

Smoked trout pâté

2 whole smoked trout
scant 1 cup cream cheese
2 tablespoons finely chopped dill
juice of ½ lemon
pinch of cayenne pepper
crackers, for serving
lemon wedges, for serving

Fish substitution
4 smoked trout fillets, skinned

Skin the smoked trout, remove the heads and skin, then lift the flesh off the bones. Break the flesh into flakes and put in a bowl or food processor. Either mash the flesh with a fork or briefly process until it is broken up but still has plenty of texture.

Beat the cream cheese with a wooden spoon until soft. Add the smoked trout flesh and mix everything together well. Stir in the dill and lemon juice, then season with salt, pepper, and cayenne pepper.

Chill the pâté until you need it but bring it to room temperature before serving or the cream cheese may cause it to become too solid. Serve with crackers. Provide extra lemon wedges to squeeze on top.

Serves 6

Oysters with vinegar and shallots

24 oysters, shucked, in their shells
1 French shallot, finely chopped
2 tablespoons red wine vinegar
rye bread and butter, for serving
 (optional)

Nestle the opened oysters on a bed of crushed ice or rock salt on a large platter (this will keep them steady).

Mix the chopped shallot with the red wine vinegar and some freshly ground black pepper in a small bowl. Put this in the center of the platter. The oysters are eaten with a little of the vinegar and shallots poured over them. Serve with buttered rye bread, if desired.

Serves 4

Garlic shrimp

2 lb. 12 oz. shrimp, peeled and
  deveined, tails intact
6 tablespoons butter, melted
$^3/_4$ cup olive oil
8 garlic cloves, crushed
2 scallions, thinly sliced
crusty bread, for serving

Preheat the oven to 500°F. Cut a slit
down the back of each shrimp.

Combine the butter and oil and divide
among four 2-cup cast-iron pots.
Divide half the crushed garlic among
the pots.

Place the pots on a baking tray and
heat in the oven for 4 minutes or until
the mixture is bubbling. Remove and
divide the shrimp and remaining garlic
among the pots. Return to the oven
for 5 minutes or until the shrimp are
cooked. Stir in the scallions. Season
to taste. Serve with crusty bread to
mop up the juices.

Serves 4

Steamed shrimp banana leaf cups

16 (4-inch) circles of banana leaf or
   8 ramekins, each with capacity of
   ½ cup
10½ oz. shrimp, peeled and deveined
1 small red chili, deseeded
2 teaspoons red curry paste
1¼-inch piece of lemongrass,
   roughly chopped
1 large egg
¼ cup coconut cream
1 tablespoon fish sauce
¼ teaspoon sugar
2 tablespoons unsalted peanuts

Begin by making eight banana leaf cups. Place two banana leaf circles together to make a double layer. Make four small tucks around the circle, stapling them to secure as you go, to create a banana leaf "cup." Repeat for the other seven cups. Alternatively, you can use eight ½-cup ramekins. Either way, also cut out eight 2¾-inch circles of baking parchment.

Put the shrimp in a food processor with the chili, lemongrass, curry paste, egg, coconut cream, fish sauce, sugar, and half of the peanuts. Blend to a rough paste.

Evenly divide the mixture among the cups. Place a circle of baking parchment on the top of each one. Place in a bamboo or metal steamer, cover, and steam for 10–12 minutes or until the mixture has risen and feels firm to the touch. You may need to cook in two batches. Remove the baking parchment.

Meanwhile, lightly toast the remaining peanuts. Cool a little, then roughly chop. Serve each cup with a little of the toasted peanuts sprinkled over the top.

Makes 8

Everyday

Marinated and seared tuna

⅓ cup soy sauce
¼ cup mirin
1 tablespoon sake
1 teaspoon superfine sugar
1 teaspoon finely grated fresh ginger
2 teaspoons lemon juice
4 (6-oz.) tuna steaks
1 tablespoon vegetable oil
cilantro leaves, for garnish

Fish substitution
   salmon

Mix the soy sauce, mirin, sake, sugar, ginger, and lemon juice together in a small bowl. Put the tuna steaks in a shallow dish and spoon the marinade on top. Turn the fish in the marinade, making sure it is well coated. Cover and leave to marinate for 30 minutes in the fridge.

Preheat a grill pan or barbecue until hot. Lift the tuna out of the marinade and pour the marinade into a small saucepan. Bring the marinade to a boil and reduce for 1 minute.

Meanwhile, lightly oil the surface of the grill pan and add the tuna steaks. Cook for 2–3 minutes on each side so that the tuna is cooked on the outside but still pink in the middle. Serve with some of the marinade spooned over the top and garnished with cilantro. Great with rice and steamed vegetables.

Serves 4

Tandoori shrimp pizza

1 tablespoon olive oil
2 teaspoons ground paprika
1/2 teaspoon ground cumin
1/4 teaspoon ground cardamom
1/4 teaspoon ground ginger
1/4 teaspoon cayenne pepper
1/3 cup yogurt, plus extra for serving
1 teaspoon lemon juice
2 garlic cloves, crushed
16 shrimp, peeled and deveined,
  tails intact
12-inch ready-made pizza crust
1 onion, sliced
1 small red pepper, sliced
3 tablespoons torn basil

Preheat the oven to 425°F. To make the tandoori sauce, heat the oil in a frying pan over medium heat, add the spices, and cook until the oil starts to bubble, then cook for another minute. Stir in the yogurt, lemon juice, and garlic, then add the shrimp. Cook for 5 minutes or until the shrimp are pink and cooked.

Remove the shrimp from the tandoori sauce with a slotted spoon and spread the sauce over the pizza crust, leaving a 1/2-inch border. Sprinkle with some of the onion and red pepper, then arrange all the shrimp on top. Top with the remaining onion and red pepper and bake for about 20 minutes. Sprinkle with basil, then serve with the extra yogurt.

Serves 4

John Dory with tarator sauce

Tarator sauce
1 cup hazelnuts
2 slices of white bread, crusts removed
2 garlic cloves, roughly crushed
1/4 cup plus 2 tablespoons olive oil, plus a little extra for cooking
1/4 cup lemon juice

1 lb. 12 oz. skinless John Dory fillets
lemon wedges, for serving

Fish substitution

grouper, snapper, halibut, cod, sea bass

To make the tarator sauce, put the hazelnuts in a food processor and grind finely. Briefly soak the bread in a small bowl of water. Squeeze dry, tear into pieces, and add to the food processor bowl along with the garlic. Process briefly to combine. Mix the oil and lemon juice together in a cup and, with the processor motor running, gradually pour it into the bread and nut mixture. Season to taste with salt and pepper, then scoop the sauce into a serving bowl.

Heat a frying pan until hot. Brush with a little oil and cook the fillets for 3 minutes on each side or until the flesh is opaque and flakes easily. You may need to cook the fish in two batches; if so, keep the first batch warm, covered with foil, in a 200°F oven. Serve the fish fillets with the tarator sauce and lemon wedges.

Serves 6

Note: Tarator sauce has its origins in Turkey. It is creamy and garlicky and can be made with walnuts, almonds, or pine nuts instead of hazelnuts.

Blackened snapper

6 large, skinless snapper fillets,
 3/4 inch thick
1/2 cup unsalted butter, melted
2 tablespoons Cajun spice mix
2 teaspoons sweet paprika
lemon wedges, for serving

Fish substitution
 blue-eye cod, mahimahi

Brush each fish fillet liberally with the melted butter.

Combine the Cajun spice mix and paprika, then sprinkle thickly over the fish. Use your fingers to rub the spice mix evenly over the fillets.

Heat a large frying pan over high heat. Cook two fillets at a time in the pan for 1–2 minutes on one side. Turn and cook for another few minutes or until the fish is cooked and flakes easily. The surface should be well charred on each side. Add extra butter if necessary. Serve drizzled with any remaining melted butter and lemon wedges—they can be served lightly charred if you like.

Serves 6

Swordfish with bananas

2 tablespoons vegetable oil
1 onion, thinly sliced
1 small green pepper, sliced
pinch of dried chili flakes
pinch of freshly grated nutmeg
2 tomatoes
2 bananas
4 (7-oz.) swordfish steaks
1 cup coconut milk
cilantro leaves, for garnish

Fish substitution
tuna, halibut

Heat the oil in a large, deep frying pan, then add the onion. Cook for 5 minutes, then add the green pepper, chili flakes, and nutmeg and cook for another 3–4 minutes or until the onion and pepper are soft.

Meanwhile, score a cross in the base of each tomato. Cover with boiling water for 30 seconds, then plunge the tomatoes into cold water. Drain and peel the skin away from the cross. Cut each tomato into quarters. Peel the bananas and cut diagonally into chunks.

Put the swordfish steaks in the pan on top of the onions and pepper and spread the tomato quarters and banana over the top. Pour the coconut milk into the pan and season with salt and pepper. Cover and cook gently for 15 minutes or until the fish is cooked through (it should feel firm when it is ready). Garnish with cilantro leaves and serve with rice.

Serves 4

Idaho trout parcels

2 tablespoons butter
1 tablespoon olive oil, plus a little for
 the parcels
1 French shallot, finely chopped
2 cups small mushrooms, sliced
2 tablespoons tarragon vinegar
1 tablespoon chopped tarragon
4 (7-oz.) pieces of skinless trout

Fish substitution

John Dory, snapper, orange roughy

Preheat the oven to 425°F. Heat the butter and oil in a frying pan, then cook the shallot for 2–3 minutes or until softened. Add the mushrooms, then stir to coat them in the oil and butter and cook for 5 minutes, stirring every now and then. Splash in the vinegar and simmer for 30 seconds. Take the pan off the heat and stir in the tarragon. Season with salt and freshly ground black pepper.

Lightly oil four 14-inch circles of heavy-duty baking parchment. Fold in half to make a crease in the middle and then unfold again. Lay them oil-side up. Put a piece of fish on one half of each circle. Top with the mushroom mixture, dividing it equally among the circles. Fold the empty half of the circle over the fish and fold the edges of the circle twice and pinch together to seal firmly. Do the same for each circle. Lay the parcels on a large baking tray and bake for 10–15 minutes. Transfer the parcels to serving plates and let everyone open his or her own.

Serves 4

Fish Provençal

1 small red pepper, thinly sliced
1 cup pasta sauce from a jar
1 tablespoon chopped thyme
3 tablespoons butter
4 large, skinless perch fillets
thyme sprigs, for garnish

Fish substitution
  snapper

Put the pepper, pasta sauce, and chopped thyme in a bowl and mix well.

Melt half the butter in a large, nonstick frying pan over high heat and cook the fish for 1 minute, adding the remaining butter during cooking. Turn the fish over and pour the pepper mixture on top. Simmer for 10 minutes or until the fish is cooked. Season to taste and garnish with thyme sprigs. Serve with roasted potato slices and crusty bread to soak up the juices.

Serves 4

Baked swordfish steaks with salsa verde

4 (7-oz.) swordfish steaks

Salsa verde
2 tablespoons olive oil
1 large onion, finely chopped
1 garlic clove, finely chopped
1 large green pepper
1½ oz. jalapeño chilies
2 tablespoons roughly chopped
   cilantro leaves

Fish substitution
   tuna, marlin, kingfish, barramundi

Preheat the oven to 350°F. Put the swordfish steaks in a large, rectangular ovenproof dish.

To make the salsa verde, heat 1 tablespoon of the oil in a small saucepan and, when hot, add the onion and garlic and cook for 10 minutes or until the onion has softened. Allow to cool for a few minutes. Blanch the pepper in boiling water for 8 minutes, then drain and chop roughly. Put the softened onion and garlic in a food processor with the pepper, chilies, cilantro, and remaining oil. Blend to a puree and season with salt. Alternatively, finely chop the ingredients by hand and mix together well.

Spread the salsa verde on top of the swordfish steaks, dividing it equally. Bake in the preheated oven for 20–25 minutes or until the fish is firm and opaque. Serve with crispy baked potato chunks.

Serves 4

Fish pie

Potato topping
3 medium floury potatoes (such as
  russet), diced
¼ cup milk or cream
1 egg, lightly beaten
2 tablespoons butter
1 cup finely shredded cheddar cheese

1 lb. 12 oz. skinless cod fillets, cut
  into large chunks
1½ cups milk
2 tablespoons butter
1 onion, finely chopped
1 garlic clove, crushed
2 tablespoons all-purpose flour
2 tablespoons lemon juice
2 teaspoons lemon zest
1 tablespoon chopped dill

Fish substitution
  snapper, monkfish, ling, haddock,
  flathead

Preheat the oven to 350°F. To make the topping, steam the potatoes until tender. Mash, then push to one side of the pan, add the milk, and heat gently. Beat the milk into the potatoes until they are fluffy, then season and stir in the egg and butter. Mix in half the cheddar, then set aside and keep warm.

Put the fish in a frying pan and cover with the milk. Bring to a boil, then reduce the heat and simmer for 2 minutes or until the fish is opaque and flaky. Drain, reserving the milk, and put the fish in a 6-cup ovenproof dish.

Melt the butter in a saucepan and cook the onion and garlic for 2 minutes. Stir in the flour and cook for 1 minute or until pale and foaming. Remove from the heat and gradually stir in the reserved milk. Return to the heat and stir constantly until it boils and thickens. Reduce the heat and simmer for 2 minutes. Add the lemon juice, zest, and dill, then season to taste. Mix with the fish. Spoon the topping over the fish and top with the remaining cheddar. Bake for 35 minutes or until golden.

Serves 4

Jansson's temptation

15 anchovy fillets
⅓ cup milk
5 tablespoons butter
2 large onions, thinly sliced
5 potatoes, peeled, cut into ¼-inch
    slices, then julienned
2 cups heavy cream

Preheat the oven to 400°F. Soak the anchovies in the milk for 5 minutes to lessen their saltiness. Drain and rinse.

Melt half the butter in a frying pan and cook the onion over medium heat for 5 minutes or until golden and tender. Chop the remaining butter into small cubes and set aside.

Spread half the potatoes over the base of a shallow, ovenproof dish, top with the anchovies and onion, and finish with the remaining potatoes.

Pour half the cream over the potatoes and sprinkle the butter cubes on top. Bake for 20 minutes or until golden. Pour the remaining cream over the top and cook for another 40 minutes or until the potatoes feel tender when the point of a knife is inserted. Season with salt and pepper before serving.

Serves 4

Stir-fried swordfish with bok choy

1 lb. 2 oz. swordfish steaks, cut into bite-size pieces
2 tablespoons freshly ground black pepper
2 tablespoons hoisin sauce
2 tablespoons rice wine
1 tablespoon oyster sauce
1 tablespoon soy sauce
vegetable oil, for cooking
3 garlic cloves, thinly sliced
1 onion, sliced
2 lb. 4 oz. baby bok choy, leaves separated
1 cup fresh shiitake mushrooms, sliced
1 tablespoon sesame seeds, toasted
1 teaspoon sesame oil

Fish substitution
  tuna

Coat the swordfish in the black pepper, then shake off any excess.

Combine the hoisin sauce, rice wine, oyster sauce, and soy sauce in a small bowl.

Heat a wok over high heat, add 2 tablespoons of the oil, and swirl it around to coat the side of the wok. Stir-fry the swordfish in batches for 1–2 minutes per batch or until tender. Be careful not to overcook the fish or it will break up. Remove from the wok.

Reheat the wok, add 1 tablespoon of the oil, then stir-fry the garlic for 30 seconds or until crisp and golden. Add the onion and stir-fry for 1–2 minutes or until golden. Add the bok choy and mushrooms and cook briefly until the leaves wilt. Pour the sauce into the wok and stir until everything is coated in the sauce.

Return the swordfish to the wok and toss everything together. Serve sprinkled with sesame seeds and drizzled with the sesame oil.

Serves 4

Mexican baked fish

3 tomatoes, chopped
½ teaspoon ground cumin
½ teaspoon ground allspice
½ teaspoon ground cinnamon
1 habanero chili, deseeded and
  finely chopped
4 tablespoons cilantro leaves
4 (6-oz.) skinless red snapper fillets
½ small red onion, chopped
½ small green pepper, chopped
1 tablespoon sour or Seville orange
  juice, or 2 teaspoons orange juice
  and 2 teaspoons vinegar
juice of 1 lime

Fish substitution
  shark, grouper, cod

Preheat the oven to 375°F. Mix the tomatoes in a bowl with the cumin, allspice, cinnamon, chili, and cilantro.

Cut four squares of foil, each large enough to enclose a fish fillet. Put a piece of fish on each of the foil squares and divide the tomato mixture among the four fillets.

Mix the red onion and green pepper together and divide among the parcels. Stir the orange and lime juices together and drizzle over the top of the fish and vegetables. Season with salt and pepper.

Wrap the fish in the foil and transfer the parcels to a baking dish. Bake for 15–20 minutes or until the fish flakes easily when tested with a fork.

Serves 4

Baked bream with fennel

4 small fennel bulbs
3 tablespoons butter
2 tablespoons olive oil
2 onions, chopped
1 garlic clove, crushed
4 (10½-oz.) whole bream, scaled
  and gutted
extra-virgin olive oil
1 lemon, quartered
1 tablespoon oregano leaves
lemon wedges, for serving

Fish substitution

1 whole sea bass (cook for an
extra 10 minutes)

Preheat the oven to 375°F and grease a large, shallow ovenproof dish. Thinly slice the fennel, reserving the green fronds.

Heat the butter and olive oil in a large frying pan and gently cook the fennel, onion, and garlic for 12–15 minutes or until softened but not browned. Season with salt and freshly ground black pepper.

Stuff each fish with a heaping tablespoon of the fennel mixture and a quarter of the fennel fronds. Brush with extra-virgin olive oil, squeeze lemon over the top, and season well.

Spoon the remainder of the fennel mixture into the ovenproof dish and sprinkle with half of the oregano. Lay the fish on top of the fennel. Sprinkle the remaining oregano over the fish and cover the dish loosely with foil. Bake for 15 minutes or until just cooked through. Garnish each serving with a wedge of lemon.

Serves 4

Pan-fried rainbow trout with almonds

2 rainbow trout, scaled and gutted
all-purpose flour, for coating
5 tablespoons butter
1 tablespoon vegetable oil
1/4 cup flaked almonds
2 tablespoons lemon juice
1 tablespoon finely chopped parsley,
   plus some extra leaves for garnish
lemon wedges, for serving

Fish substitution
   any type of trout

Wash the fish and pat dry with paper towels. Coat the fish with flour and season well on each side as well as inside. Heat half the butter and all of the oil in a large frying pan until it is very hot, then add the fish. Cook for 4 minutes on each side or until golden brown and cooked through. Lift up one side of the fish to check if the flesh on the inside is opaque and cooked through. If cooked, the dorsal fin should pull out easily. Remove the fish and place on warm serving plates. Cover very loosely with foil and place in a warm oven.

Heat the remaining butter in a frying pan, add the flaked almonds, and stir until the almonds turn light golden. Add the lemon juice and parsley and season with salt and pepper. Stir until the sauce is heated through. Pour over the fish, garnish with parsley, then serve with lemon wedges.

Serves 2

Basic pan-fried fish

2–3 tablespoons all-purpose flour
4 blue-eye cod cutlets
olive oil, for shallow-frying

Fish substitution
  warehou, snapper, other types
  of cod

Sift the flour together with a little salt and freshly ground black pepper on a plate. Pat the fish dry with paper towels, then coat both sides of the cutlets with the seasoned flour, shaking off any excess.

Heat about ⅛ inch of oil in a large frying pan until very hot. Put the fish into the hot oil and cook for 3 minutes on one side, then turn and cook the other side for 2 minutes or until the coating is crisp and well browned. Reduce the heat to low and cook for another 2–3 minutes or until the flesh flakes easily when tested with a fork.

Remove the fish from the pan and drain briefly on crumpled paper towels. If you are cooking in batches, keep warm while cooking the remaining cutlets. Serve immediately with a salad or steamed vegetables.

Serves 4

Fresh tuna and green bean stir-fry

2 cups small green beans, trimmed
2 tablespoons vegetable oil
1 lb. 5 oz. piece of tuna, cut into
　small cubes
9 oz. small cherry tomatoes
16 small black olives
2–3 tablespoons lemon juice
2 garlic cloves, finely chopped
8 anchovy fillets, rinsed, dried, and
　finely chopped
3 tablespoons small basil leaves

Blanch the beans in a small saucepan of boiling water for 2 minutes. Drain and rinse under cold water, then set aside.

Heat a wok until very hot, add the oil, and swirl it around to coat the side. Stir-fry the tuna in batches for about 5 minutes per batch or until cooked on the outside but still a little pink on the inside.

Add the cherry tomatoes, olives, and beans to the wok, then gently toss until heated through. Add the lemon juice, garlic, and anchovies and stir well. Season to taste with salt and freshly ground black pepper. Serve sprinkled with the basil leaves.

Serves 4

Roast fish with rosemary and garlic

2 lb. 4 oz. skinless monkfish tail fillets,
    membrane removed
3 large garlic cloves, peeled and
    sliced into thin slivers
1 stem of rosemary, cut into
    24 small sprigs
6 bacon strips, cut in half
1/3 cup olive oil
lemon wedges, for serving

Fish substitution
    cod, halibut, swordfish, barramundi

Preheat the oven to 400°F. Using a small, sharp knife, make small incisions in the fish and insert a sliver of garlic and a small sprig of rosemary into each one. Season the fish with salt and pepper and wrap a piece of bacon around each piece of fish.

Put the fish in a roasting pan and drizzle the olive oil on top. Roast for about 15 minutes or until the fish is cooked through. Serve with lemon wedges.

Serves 4

African fish pie

2 tablespoons butter, plus a little
  extra for greasing the pan
2 onions, finely chopped
2 garlic cloves, crushed
2 tablespoons mild curry powder
1/2 teaspoon turmeric
grated zest and juice of 1 small lemon
1/2 cup raisins
1/3 cup whole blanched almonds,
  chopped
1 cup milk
2 thick slices white bread
2 lb. 4 oz. skinless cod fillet, finely
  chopped
2 large eggs

Fish substitution
  pike, snook

Preheat the oven to 375°F. Heat the butter in a frying pan and add the onion. Cook for 7–8 minutes or until soft and lightly golden, stirring occasionally. Add the garlic and cook for another 2 minutes. Mix in 1 tablespoon of the curry powder, the turmeric, lemon zest and juice, raisins, and almonds. Remove from the heat and allow to cool for 10 minutes.

Pour 2 1/2 tablespoons of the milk into a bowl and soak the bread in it for 10 minutes, turning after 5 minutes. Squeeze the bread dry, then tear into small pieces and put in a bowl. Add the fish, one of the eggs, and the mixture from the frying pan to the bowl, season well, and mix together. Scoop into a lightly buttered, 9-inch square nonstick pan that is 2 3/4 inches high. Bake for 15 minutes. Toward the end of the baking time, whisk together the remaining milk, curry powder, and egg. Pour the liquid over the top of the mixture in the pan. Bake for another 45 minutes or until set. Cool for 15 minutes, then cut into squares to serve.

Serves 6

Steamed fish cutlets with ginger and chili

4 (6-oz.) firm grouper cutlets
2-inch piece of fresh ginger, shredded
2 garlic cloves, chopped
2 teaspoons chopped red chilies
2 tablespoons chopped cilantro stalks
3 scallions, cut into fine, short shreds
2 tablespoons lime juice

Fish substitution
  snapper, cod

Line a bamboo steamer basket with banana leaves or baking parchment to prevent the fish from sticking to the base.

Arrange the fish in the steamer and top with the ginger, garlic, chilies, and cilantro stalks. Cover and steam over a wok or pan of boiling water for 8–10 minutes or until the fish flakes easily. Sprinkle the scallions and lime juice over the fish, cover, and steam for an extra 30 seconds. Serve with steamed jasmine rice.

Serves 4

Baked tuna Siciliana

1/3 cup olive oil

2 tablespoons lemon juice

2 1/2 tablespoons finely chopped basil

4 (6-oz.) tuna steaks

1/4 cup pitted and chopped black
olives

1 tablespoon baby capers, rinsed
and patted dry

2 anchovies, finely chopped

3 medium tomatoes, peeled,
deseeded, and chopped, or a
14-oz. can of chopped tomatoes

2 tablespoons dry bread crumbs

bread, for serving

Fish substitution
swordfish

Mix 2 tablespoons of the olive oil with the lemon juice and 1 tablespoon of the basil. Season and pour into a shallow, nonmetallic ovenproof dish, large enough to hold the tuna steaks in a single layer. Arrange the tuna in the dish and leave to marinate for 15 minutes, turning once. Preheat the oven to 425°F.

Combine the olives, capers, anchovies, and tomatoes with the remaining oil and basil and season well. Spread over the tuna and sprinkle the bread crumbs over the top. Bake for about 20 minutes or until the fish is just opaque. Finish off by placing briefly under a broiler until the bread crumbs are crisp. Serve with bread to soak up the juices.

Serves 4

Baked Atlantic salmon

16 cherry tomatoes, cut in half
3/4 cup fresh, ripe pineapple flesh,
   diced
4 (7-oz.) Atlantic salmon fillets, skin
   left on
2 tablespoons balsamic vinegar
2 tablespoons olive oil
3½ oz. arugula or baby spinach
4 tablespoons shredded basil leaves

Fish substitution
   kingfish, large trout fillets, cod

Preheat the oven to 350°F. Mix the tomatoes and pineapple together.

Line a baking tray with a piece of foil. Place the salmon fillets on the foil and season with salt and pepper. Spoon the tomato and pineapple mixture on top of the fillets, dividing it equally. Whisk the balsamic vinegar and olive oil together in a small bowl and drizzle over the top. Wrap the parcel to enclose the fish and bake for 20–25 minutes or until the salmon is opaque but still moist and succulent.

Make a small bed of arugula or spinach leaves in the center of each plate. Lift the salmon fillets out of the foil and place on top of the leaves. Spoon on the pineapple and tomato mixture, drizzle with the cooking juices, and sprinkle with basil.

Serves 4

Crunchy fish fillets with chive mayonnaise

2/3 cup mayonnaise
2 tablespoons chopped chives
1 tablespoon sweet chili sauce
1/2 cup cornmeal
4 (7-oz.) skinless perch fillets
1/4 cup vegetable oil

Fish substitution
   snapper, John Dory, whiting,
   haddock, cod

For the chive mayonnaise, combine the mayonnaise, chives, and chili sauce in a small bowl. Keep refrigerated until needed.

Put the cornmeal on a plate. Score four diagonal slashes in the skin side of each fish fillet to keep the fish from curling during cooking. Press both sides of the fillets into the cornmeal to coat thoroughly.

Heat the oil in a frying pan over medium heat. Add the fish and cook for 3 minutes. Turn and cook for another 3 minutes or until tender and the fish flakes easily when tested with a fork. Remove and drain on crumpled paper towels. Serve with the chive mayonnaise.

Serves 4

Steamed whole snapper with Asian flavors

1 lb. 12 oz. whole snapper, scaled
    and gutted
3 stems of lemongrass
handful of cilantro leaves
small knob of fresh ginger, peeled
    and julienned
1 large garlic clove, peeled and cut
    into thin slivers
2 tablespoons soy sauce
¼ cup vegetable oil
1 tablespoon fish sauce
1 small red chili, deseeded and
    finely chopped

Fish substitution
    coral trout, sea bass

Score the fish with diagonal cuts on both sides. Cut each stem of lemongrass into thirds and lightly squash each piece with the end of the handle of a large knife. Put half of the lemongrass in the middle of a large piece of foil and lay the fish on top. Put the remaining lemongrass and half of the cilantro inside the cavity of the fish.

Mix the ginger, garlic, soy sauce, oil, fish sauce, and chili together. Drizzle the mixture over the fish and sprinkle with the remaining cilantro.

Enclose the fish in the foil and place in a large bamboo or metal steamer over a pan of simmering water. Steam for 25 minutes or until the flesh of the fish is opaque and white. Serve with stir-fried vegetables and rice.

Serves 2

Fish burgers and crunchy potato wedges

1 lb. 2 oz. skinless cod fillets
2 tablespoons finely chopped parsley
2 tablespoons finely chopped dill
2 tablespoons lemon juice
1 tablespoon capers, drained, rinsed, and chopped
2 gherkins, finely chopped
2 large potatoes, cooked and mashed
all-purpose flour, for dusting
1 tablespoon olive oil
4 hamburger buns, split into halves
lettuce leaves
2 Roma tomatoes, sliced
tartar sauce, for serving

Crunchy potato wedges
6 potatoes
1 tablespoon vegetable oil, plus extra for deep-frying
½ teaspoon salt
¼ cup dry bread crumbs
2 teaspoons chopped chives
1 teaspoon celery salt
¼ teaspoon garlic powder
½ teaspoon chopped rosemary

Fish substitution
ling, redfish, warehou

Put the fish fillets in a frying pan and add enough water so that the fish is just covered. Slowly heat the water, making sure it doesn't come to a boil. Cover with a lid and cook over low heat until the fish is just cooked through. Drain the fish on crumpled paper towels, then transfer to a bowl and flake the flesh with a fork, removing any bones.

Add the parsley, dill, lemon juice, capers, gherkins, and potatoes to the bowl with the fish, then season with freshly ground black pepper and some salt and mix well. Divide the mixture into four portions and shape each into a patty. Lightly dust the patties with flour, cover, and refrigerate for 1 hour— this will help them stick together during cooking.

In the meantime, make the potato wedges. Preheat the oven to 400°F. Wash the potatoes, then cut them into wedges, leaving the skin on. Pat the potato wedges dry with paper towels and then toss with the oil so they are all covered. Combine the salt, bread crumbs, chives, celery salt, garlic powder, and rosemary and then toss with the wedges. Spread the wedges out onto a greased baking tray and bake for 40 minutes or until golden.

Heat the oil in a large, nonstick frying pan, add the fish patties, and cook for 5–6 minutes on each side or until well browned and cooked through.

Grill the buns and butter them if you wish. On each base, put some lettuce, tomato, a fish patty, and some tartar sauce. Top with the other half of the bun and serve with the crunchy potato wedges.

Serves 4

Steamed trout with soy, rice wine, and ginger

2 (8-oz.) rainbow trout, scaled
  and gutted
¼ cup soy sauce
½ teaspoon sesame oil
1 teaspoon rice vinegar or white
  wine vinegar
2 teaspoons rice wine or dry sherry
1 tablespoon finely shredded fresh
  ginger
2 tablespoons chopped cilantro
2 scallions, finely chopped

Fish substitution
  sea bass, bream

Rinse the fish and pat dry with paper towels. Score both sides of each fish three times and place the fish in a shallow, ovenproof dish.

Mix together the soy sauce, sesame oil, vinegar, rice wine, and ginger. Pour some of the soy sauce mixture inside the fish and then pour the rest on top of the fish.

Place the dish in a large bamboo or metal steamer set over a pan of simmering water. Cover and steam for 15 minutes or until the flesh of the fish is opaque—lift up one side of each fish and look inside to see if the flesh around the spine is opaque. If not, cook until it is.

Take off the lid and sprinkle the cilantro and scallions over each fish. Serve with rice.

Serves 2

Red emperor poached in coconut milk

4 cups coconut milk
2 teaspoons grated fresh ginger
3 small red chilies, finely chopped
1 tablespoon chopped cilantro roots
    and stems
6 red Asian shallots, finely chopped
6 kaffir lime leaves, shredded
2 stems of lemongrass, white part
    only, sliced
2 teaspoons grated lime zest
2 cups fish stock
1/3 cup fish sauce
1/3 cup lime juice, strained
4 (9-oz.) skinless red emperor fillets,
    each fillet cut into three equal
    portions
cilantro leaves, for garnish
1 small red chili, cut in long strips,
    for garnish
2 kaffir lime leaves, extra, shredded,
    for garnish

Fish substitution
    coral trout, snapper, cod

Bring the coconut milk to a boil in a saucepan and boil for 3 minutes. Add the ginger, chilies, cilantro roots and stems, shallots, lime leaves, lemongrass, and lime zest and bring back to a boil. Add the fish stock and fish sauce and simmer for 15 minutes. Pass through a fine strainer and add the lime juice. Taste and add extra fish sauce if necessary.

Heat the sauce in a large frying pan. When the sauce comes to a boil, add the fish, then reduce the heat and simmer very gently for 10–15 minutes or until just cooked through.

Carefully transfer the fish to a serving platter. Serve with some of the liquid and a sprinkling of cilantro, chili, and shreds of lime leaf.

Serves 4

Seafood mornay

6 tablespoons butter
½ cup all-purpose flour
½ cup dry white wine
1 cup heavy cream
1 cup milk
1 cup cheddar cheese, grated
2 tablespoons whole-grain mustard
1 tablespoon horseradish
6 scallions, chopped
1 cup fresh bread crumbs
2 lb. 4 oz. skinless monkfish fillets,
  cut into cubes
1 lb. scallops, cleaned
14 oz. small shrimp, cooked and
  peeled

Topping
3 cups fresh bread crumbs
3 tablespoons chopped parsley
5 tablespoons butter, melted
1 cup shredded cheddar cheese

Fish substitution
  snapper, flathead

Preheat the oven to 350°F. Lightly grease an 8-cup ovenproof dish. Melt 4 tablespoons of the butter in a saucepan over low heat. Stir in the flour until pale and foaming. Remove the pan from the heat and gradually stir in the wine, cream, and milk. Return the pan to the heat and stir over high heat until the sauce boils and thickens. Season to taste with salt and pepper. Add the cheddar, mustard, horseradish, scallions, and bread crumbs. Mix well and set aside.

Melt the remaining butter in a large pan and add the fish and scallops in batches. Stir over low heat until the seafood starts to change color. Drain the seafood, add to the sauce with the shrimp, then transfer to the greased dish.

For the topping, mix all the ingredients and spread over the seafood. Bake the mornay for 35 minutes or until the top is golden and the sauce bubbling.

Serves 8–10

Piri piri shrimp

½ cup vegetable oil
2 teaspoons dried chili flakes
4 large garlic cloves, crushed
2 lb. 4 oz. shrimp, peeled and
  deveined, tails intact
5 tablespoons butter
¼ cup lemon juice

Put the oil, chili flakes, garlic, and
1 teaspoon salt in a large, nonmetallic
bowl and mix well. Add the shrimp
and coat them in the mixture.
Refrigerate for 3 hours, stirring and
turning occasionally.

Preheat the broiler to very hot. Put the
shrimp in a single layer on a baking
tray and brush with the remaining
oil and chili mixture. Broil for about
5 minutes or until cooked through,
turning once.

Meanwhile, melt the butter with the
lemon juice in a small saucepan.
Serve the shrimp hot, drizzled with
the lemon juice and butter mixture
and accompanied by rice.

Serves 4

Winter

Tom yum goong

1 tablespoon vegetable oil
1 lb. 2 oz. shrimp, peeled and
  deveined, reserving the heads
  and shells
2 tablespoons Thai red curry paste
  or tom yum paste
2 tablespoons tamarind puree
  (see Note)
2 teaspoons ground turmeric
1 teaspoon chopped red chilies
4 kaffir lime leaves, shredded
2 tablespoons fish sauce
2 tablespoons lime juice
2 teaspoons brown sugar
2 tablespoons cilantro leaves

Heat the oil in a large saucepan or wok and cook the shrimp heads and shells for 10 minutes over medium heat, stirring frequently, until the heads are deep orange in color.

Add 1 cup water and the curry paste to the saucepan. Bring to a boil and cook for 5 minutes or until reduced slightly. Add another 8 cups water and simmer for 20 minutes. Strain, discarding the shells and heads, and pour the stock back into the pan.

Add the tamarind, turmeric, chilies, and lime leaves to the saucepan, bring to a boil, and cook for 2 minutes. Add the shrimp and cook for 5 minutes or until pink. Stir in the fish sauce, lime juice, and sugar. Serve sprinkled with cilantro leaves.

Serves 4–6

Note: If you are unable to find tamarind puree, you can make your own by soaking an 8-oz. packet of tamarind pulp in 2 cups boiling water for 1–2 hours, crushing occasionally. Push through a sieve and discard the pulp. Alternatively, use lemon juice.

Tunisian fish soup

¼ cup olive oil
1 onion, chopped
1 celery stalk, chopped
4 garlic cloves, crushed
2 tablespoons tomato paste
1½ teaspoons ground turmeric
1½ teaspoons ground cumin
2 teaspoons harissa
4 cups fish stock
2 bay leaves
1 cup orzo or other small pasta
1 lb. 2 oz. mixed skinless snapper
and sea bass fillets, cut into bite-
size chunks
2 tablespoons chopped mint, plus
some extra leaves for garnish
2 tablespoons lemon juice

Fish substitution
cod, haddock, ocean perch,
coral trout

Heat the oil in a large saucepan, add the onion and celery, and cook for 8–10 minutes or until softened. Add the garlic and cook for another minute. Stir in the tomato paste, turmeric, cumin, and harissa and cook, stirring constantly, for another 30 seconds.

Pour the fish stock into the saucepan and add the bay leaves. Bring the liquid to a boil, then reduce the heat to low and simmer gently for 15 minutes.

Add the orzo to the liquid and cook for 2–3 minutes or until al dente. Drop the chunks of fish into the liquid and poach gently for 3–4 minutes or until the fish is opaque. Remove the bay leaves, stir in the mint and lemon juice, season to taste with salt, then serve with warm pita bread. Garnish with mint leaves.

Serves 6

Bourride

Garlic croutons
½ stale baguette, sliced
¼ cup olive oil
1 garlic clove, halved

Aioli
2 egg yolks
4 garlic cloves, crushed
1–2 tablespoons lemon juice
1 cup olive oil

Stock
¼ teaspoon saffron threads
4 cups dry white wine
1 leek, white part only, chopped
2 carrots, chopped
2 onions, chopped
2 long strips of orange zest
2 teaspoons fennel seeds
3 thyme sprigs

5½ lb. monkfish fillets, skinned and
    cut into 1½-inch pieces, reserving
    the trimmings for use in the stock
3 egg yolks
thyme sprigs, for garnish

Fish substitution
    sea bass, cod, perch, sole, bream

Preheat the oven to 315°F. To make the croutons, brush the bread with oil and bake for 10 minutes or until crisp. Rub one side of each slice with garlic.

To make the aioli, put the egg yolks, garlic, and 1 tablespoon of the lemon juice in a mortar and pestle or food processor and pound or mix until light and creamy. Add the oil, drop by drop, whisking constantly until it begins to thicken, then add the oil in a very thin stream. If you're using a food processor, pour in the oil in a thin stream with the motor running. Season with salt and pepper, add the remaining lemon juice, and, if necessary, thin with a little warm water. Cover and refrigerate until you're ready to serve.

To make the stock, soak the saffron in a tablespoon of hot water for 15 minutes. Put the saffron and its soaking liquid, the wine, leek, carrot, onion, orange zest, fennel seeds, thyme, and fish trimmings in a large saucepan with 4 cups water. Cover and bring to a boil, then simmer for 20 minutes, occasionally skimming the impurities off the surface. Strain the liquid into a clean saucepan, pressing down on the solids with a wooden spoon to extract all the liquid.

Bring the stock to a gentle simmer, add half the fish pieces, and poach for 5 minutes. Remove the fish with a slotted spoon and keep warm while you cook the rest of the fish, then remove all the fish pieces from the pan and bring the stock back to a boil. Boil for 5 minutes or until slightly reduced, then remove the pan from the heat.

Put half the aioli and the three egg yolks in a large bowl and mix until smooth. Whisk in a ladleful of hot stock, then gradually add five ladlefuls, stirring constantly. Pour back into the pan with the rest of the stock and whisk over low heat for 3–5 minutes or until the soup is hot and slightly thicker (don't let it boil or it will curdle). Season with salt and pepper.

To serve, put two garlic croutons in each bowl, top with a few pieces of fish, and add the hot soup. Garnish with thyme sprigs. You can either serve the remaining aioli separately or add a dollop to the soup before you serve it.

Serves 4

Goan fish curry

4 cardamom pods
1 teaspoon coriander seeds
2 teaspoons mustard seeds
2 tablespoons shredded coconut
1/4 cup vegetable oil
1 large onion, chopped
2 garlic cloves, finely chopped
3 small green chilies, deseeded and
  finely chopped
1 tablespoon grated fresh ginger
1/2 teaspoon ground turmeric
pinch of freshly grated nutmeg
4 cloves
2 tablespoons tamarind puree
6 curry leaves
2 cinnamon sticks
3 1/2 cups coconut milk
1 lb. 5 oz. skinless pomfret fillets, cut
  into strips
12 small shrimp, peeled and deveined
cilantro leaves, for garnish

Fish substitution
  flounder, plaice, sole

Lightly crush the cardamom pods until the pods split, then remove the seeds from the pods and put in a small frying pan with the coriander seeds. Dry-fry until fragrant and the seeds begin to jump. Remove from the heat and tip into a mortar and pestle or spice grinder. Grind the seeds to a powder.

Put the mustard seeds into the frying pan with the coconut and toast together until the seeds begin to pop and the coconut turns light golden. Remove from the heat and set aside.

Heat the oil in a saucepan and add the onion. Cook for 4–5 minutes or until it starts to soften. Add the garlic, chilies, ginger, turmeric, and nutmeg and cook for another minute. Add the ground spices, the toasted coconut and mustard seeds, the cloves, tamarind, curry leaves, cinnamon sticks, and coconut milk. Stir well and heat to just below boiling point, then reduce the heat and simmer, uncovered, for 10 minutes or until slightly thickened. Add the strips of fish and the shrimp and poach for 5 minutes or until the fish is opaque and the shrimp are pale pink. Garnish with cilantro leaves.

Serves 4

Caldeirada

1 lb. 12 oz. (about 5 medium) waxy
   potatoes (such as pink fir or red),
   cut into thick slices
¼ cup olive oil
1 large onion, thinly sliced
4 large garlic cloves, finely chopped
1 red pepper, sliced
1 tablespoon paprika
1 tablespoon red wine vinegar
½ cup dry white wine
14 oz. mussels, cleaned
4 (3½-oz.) hake steaks
12 shrimp, peeled and deveined

Fish substitution
   cod, bream, sea bass

Put the potatoes in a saucepan, cover with boiling water, and bring to a boil. Reduce the heat to medium, add a pinch of salt, and simmer for 10 minutes or until tender. Drain and arrange in a serving dish, keeping warm in an oven if necessary.

Meanwhile, heat the oil in a large, wide sauté pan with a lid, then cook the onion for 5 minutes over medium heat. Add the garlic and pepper and cook for a minute, stirring. Add the paprika, vinegar, wine, and 2½ tablespoons water. Bring to a boil, add the mussels, and cover. Allow to bubble for 4 minutes (the mussels should open), then remove the mussels from the pan, discarding any that have not opened, and reduce the heat to low.

Put the fish steaks and shrimp on top of the onion mixture, cover, and cook for 7 minutes, turning both halfway through the cooking time. Return the mussels to the pan for the final minute to heat through. When cooked, the fish will be opaque and the shrimp will be pink. Season to taste. Spoon the seafood mixture over the top of the potatoes, then serve.

Serves 4

Brazilian seafood stew

4 (7-oz.) bream fillets
7 oz. large shrimp, peeled and
  deveined
2½ tablespoons lime juice
2 tablespoons olive oil
1 large onion, finely chopped
4 large garlic cloves, crushed
1 large red pepper, chopped
1 habanero chili, deseeded and
  finely chopped
3 medium ripe tomatoes
1¼ cups coconut milk
chopped cilantro leaves, for garnish
thin strips of lime zest, for garnish

Fish substitution
  mahimahi, halibut, sole, cod, bass

Put the fish and shrimp in a shallow, nonmetallic dish. Drizzle the lime juice over the top, season, then turn the seafood in the juice. Cover and marinate in the fridge for 30 minutes.

Meanwhile, heat the oil in a large saucepan and add the onion. Cook for 8–10 minutes or until softened, then add the garlic, pepper, and chili and cook for another 3 minutes, stirring now and then.

Score a cross in the base of each tomato. Soak in boiling water for 30 seconds, then plunge into cold water. Peel the skin away from the cross. Chop the tomatoes, discarding the cores. Add the tomatoes to the pan and cook for 5 minutes or until the mixture thickens. Allow to cool a little, then tip the mixture into a food processor or blender and blend until smooth. Return the sauce to the pan. Pour in the coconut milk and bring to a gentle simmer. Lift the fish and shrimp out of the dish and add to the pan, leaving behind any remaining marinade. Cook for 4 minutes or until opaque. Season and sprinkle with cilantro and lime zest.

Serves 4

Chunky fish soup with bacon and dumplings

2 tablespoons olive oil
1 onion, chopped
1 small red pepper, chopped
1 small zucchini, diced
10 strips smoked bacon, chopped
1 garlic clove, crushed
2 tablespoons paprika
14-oz. can chopped tomatoes
14-oz. can chickpeas
1 lb. skinless pike fillet, cut into
  large pieces
2 tablespoons chopped Italian
  parsley

Dumplings
1/2 cup plus 2 tablespoons
  self-rising flour
1 egg, lightly beaten
1 1/2 tablespoons milk
2 teaspoons finely chopped
  marjoram

Fish substitution
  bream, trout

Heat the oil in a large saucepan, then add the onion. Cook over low heat for 8–10 minutes or until softened. Add the pepper, zucchini, bacon, and garlic and cook over medium heat for 5 minutes, stirring now and then.

Meanwhile, make the dumpling mixture by combining the flour, egg, milk, and marjoram together in a bowl with a wooden spoon.

Add the paprika, chopped tomatoes, chickpeas, and 3 1/2 cups water to the vegetables in the saucepan. Bring the liquid to a boil, then reduce the heat to low and simmer gently for 10 minutes or until thickened slightly. Using two spoons to help you form the dumplings, add six rounds of the dumpling mixture to the soup (this should use up all the mixture). Poach for 2 minutes, then slide the pieces of fish into the liquid. Poach for another 2–3 minutes or until the fish is cooked. The dumplings and fish should be ready simultaneously. Season to taste, sprinkle with parsley, then serve.

Serves 6

Thai yellow fish curry

Paste

Paste
1 tablespoon chopped fresh turmeric
  or ½ tablespoon ground turmeric
1 teaspoon ground coriander
1 teaspoon ground cumin
3 small yellow or red chilies
1 stem of lemongrass, cut into
  3 pieces
small knob of fresh galangal or
  ginger, peeled
1 tablespoon chopped cilantro root
2 large garlic cloves, peeled
? red Asian shallots, peeled
1 teaspoon dried shrimp paste

Curry
¼ cup vegetable oil
3½ cups coconut milk
4 kaffir lime leaves (optional)
finely grated zest and juice of 1 lime
1 tablespoon fish sauce
1 teaspoon brown sugar
30 Thai pea eggplants (optional)
  (see Notes)
4 Thai or other baby eggplants,
  quartered, or 5½ oz. regular
  eggplant, cut into small chunks
1¾ oz. bean sprouts, trimmed
12 tiger shrimp, peeled and deveined,
  tails intact
1 lb. 5 oz. skinless lemon sole fillets,
  cut into bite-size chunks
2 tablespoons Thai basil or other
  basil leaves
1 tablespoon cilantro leaves

Fish substitution
  cod, hapuka, snapper, kingfish,
  grouper

To make the curry paste, put the turmeric, coriander, cumin, chilies, lemongrass, galangal, cilantro root, garlic, shallots, shrimp paste, and ¼ cup water in a food processor and whizz until it forms a thick paste. Alternatively, if you don't have a food processor, you can chop all the ingredients very finely with a sharp knife or crush them in a mortar and pestle and then mix everything together by hand.

Heat the oil in a large saucepan or wok, then add the curry paste. Cook, stirring often, for 5 minutes or until fragrant. Pour in the coconut milk, then add the lime leaves, lime zest and juice, fish sauce, sugar, Thai pea eggplants (if using), and the other eggplants. Stir well, bring the mixture to a boil, then reduce the heat to low, cover with a lid, and simmer for 15 minutes or until the curry has thickened slightly and the eggplants are cooked.

Remove the lid from the pan and add the bean sprouts, shrimp, and chunks of fish. Cook for 5 minutes or until the shrimp have turned a pale pink and the fish is opaque. Stir in the basil and cilantro, add a little salt if needed, and serve with steamed rice.

Serves 4

Notes: There are many good-quality curry pastes available in the Asian section of most supermarkets. If you'd prefer to use one of these rather than making your own, use 3–4 tablespoons yellow curry paste and skip the first step.

Thai pea eggplants are very small and round, not much bigger than a marble. They are sometimes available at Asian markets.

Russian fish soup

4 tablespoons butter
1 large onion, thinly sliced
1 celery stalk, chopped
5 tablespoons all-purpose flour
2 tablespoons tomato paste
4 cups fish stock
2 large gherkins, rinsed and chopped
1 tablespoon capers, rinsed and
   squeezed dry
1 bay leaf
¼ teaspoon freshly grated nutmeg
1 lb. 5 oz. mixed carp, perch, or
   bream fillets, skinned and cut
   into chunks
2 tablespoons chopped parsley
2 tablespoons chopped dill, plus a
   little extra for garnish
sour cream, for serving

Fish substitution
   tench, haddock, sea bass

Melt the butter in a large saucepan.
Add the onion and celery and cook
gently over low heat for 7–8 minutes
or until softened and translucent.
Increase the heat, stir in the flour
and tomato paste, and cook, stirring
constantly, for 30 seconds. Pour in
the fish stock and slowly bring to a
boil, stirring frequently.

Reduce the heat to low and add the
gherkins, capers, bay leaf, nutmeg,
and chunks of fish. Poach gently
for 2–3 minutes or until the fish is
opaque. Remove the bay leaf. Gently
stir in the parsley and dill and season
generously with salt and pepper.
Serve each bowl of soup topped
with a spoonful of sour cream and
a sprinkling of dill.

Serves 4

Penang laksa

1 lb. 12 oz. whole snapper, scaled
  and gutted
3 tablespoons tamarind puree
1 teaspoon brown sugar
4½ oz. thin dried white rice noodles
1 tablespoon vegetable oil
3½-oz. cucumber, peeled and
  julienned
2 red Asian shallots, thinly sliced
7 oz. peeled pineapple, cut into
  small chunks
1 small red chili, sliced (optional)
½ bunch Vietnamese mint, small
  leaves left whole, the rest roughly
  shredded

Curry paste
1 small onion, roughly chopped
1 teaspoon chopped fresh turmeric
1 tablespoon grated fresh ginger
2 small red chilies, roughly chopped
1 teaspoon shrimp paste

Fish substitution
  coral trout, red emperor, cod,
  sea bass

Put the whole fish in a large saucepan and cover with cold water. Add 1 teaspoon salt and bring to a boil. Cook for 10 minutes, skimming any scum that rises to the surface. Lift the fish out of the liquid. Drain the liquid, reserving 3 cups, then stir in the tamarind and sugar to make tamarind stock. Remove the bones from the fish, discarding the head and skin. Flake roughly—you should end up with 13–14 oz. of cooked fish.

To make the curry paste, put all the ingredients and 2 tablespoons water in a food processor and briefly whizz into a paste.

Soak the noodles in boiling water for 10 minutes. Drain.

Heat the oil in a large saucepan and, when sizzling, add the curry paste. Cook for 5 minutes, stirring constantly. Pour in the tamarind stock, bring to a boil, then reduce the heat and simmer for 5 minutes. Add the chunks of fish for just long enough to heat them through.

Divide the noodles among four deep bowls. Top with the cucumber, shallots, pineapple, chili (if using), and mint. Add the soup, then serve.

Serves 4

Creamy garlic seafood

6 raw slipper lobsters or crabs
4 tablespoons butter
1 onion, finely chopped
5–6 large garlic cloves, finely chopped
$1/2$ cup white wine
2 cups cream
$1 1/2$ tablespoons Dijon mustard
2 teaspoons lemon juice
1 lb. 2 oz. raw shrimp, peeled and
    deveined, tails intact
1 lb. 2 oz. skinless perch fillets, cut
    into bite-size cubes
12 scallops, with roe, cleaned
2 tablespoons chopped Italian parsley

Fish substitution

perch, ling, bream, tuna, cod

Cut the heads off the lobsters, then use scissors to cut down around the sides of the tails so you can flap open the shells. Remove the flesh in one piece.

Melt the butter in a frying pan and cook the onion and garlic over medium heat for 2 minutes or until the onion is softened. Add the wine to the pan and cook for 4 minutes or until reduced by half. Stir in the cream, mustard, and lemon juice and simmer for 5–6 minutes or until reduced by almost half.

Add the shrimp and cook for 1 minute, then add the lobster meat and cook for another minute or until opaque. Add the perch and cook for 2 minutes or until cooked through (the flesh will flake easily when tested with a fork). Finally, add the scallops and cook for 1 minute, until all the seafood is cooked. Remove the pan from the heat and toss the parsley through. Season to taste. Serve with salad and bread.

Serves 6

Japanese shrimp, scallop, and noodle soup

4 dried shiitake mushrooms
3½ oz. dried soba or somen noodles
¼-oz. sachet bonito-flavored soup
 stock
2½ oz. carrots, julienned
5½ oz. firm tofu, cut into cubes
16 shrimp, peeled and deveined, tails
 intact
8 scallops, cleaned
2 scallions, finely chopped
1 tablespoon mirin
shichimi togarashi, for serving (see
 Note)

Fish substitution

chunks of firm white fish, fish balls

Soak the mushrooms in 1¼ cups boiling water for 30 minutes. Meanwhile, cook the noodles in a pot of boiling water for 2 minutes or until just tender, then drain and rinse with cold water. Return the noodles to the pan and cover.

In a large saucepan, mix the stock with 4 cups water. Drain the mushrooms and add the soaking liquid to the pan. Chop the mushroom caps, discarding the stalks. Add the mushrooms and carrots to the pan and bring the liquid to a boil. Reduce the heat to a simmer and cook for 5 minutes. Add the tofu, shrimp, scallops, scallions, and mirin to the pan. Cook at a gentle simmer for 4 minutes or until the shrimp have turned pink and are cooked and the scallops are firm and opaque.

Meanwhile, pour hot water over the noodles and swish the noodles around to separate and warm them. Drain. Divide the noodles among four large bowls and pour the soup over them, dividing the seafood equally. Serve, offering the shichimi togarashi as a flavoring to sprinkle on top.

Serves 4

Note: Shichimi togarashi is a Japanese condiment.

Thai shrimp curry

Curry paste
1 small onion, roughly chopped
3 garlic cloves
4 dried red chilies
4 whole black peppercorns
2 tablespoons chopped lemongrass,
   white part only
1 tablespoon chopped cilantro root
2 teaspoons grated lime zest
2 teaspoons cumin seeds
1 teaspoon sweet paprika
1 teaspoon ground coriander
2 tablespoons vegetable oil

1 tablespoon vegetable oil
2 tablespoons fish sauce
3/4-inch piece of fresh galangal, thinly
   sliced
4 kaffir lime leaves
14-oz. can coconut cream
2 lb. 4 oz. shrimp, peeled and
   deveined, tails intact
sliced fresh red chilies, for garnish
   (optional)
cilantro leaves, for garnish

To make the curry paste, put all the
ingredients and 1 teaspoon salt in a
small food processor. Whizz until the
mixture forms a smooth paste.

Heat the remaining tablespoon of oil
in a pan. Add half the curry paste and
stir over low heat for 30 seconds. Add
the fish sauce, galangal, lime leaves,
and coconut cream to the pan and
stir until well combined.

Add the shrimp to the pan and
simmer, uncovered, for 10 minutes
or until the shrimp are cooked and
the sauce has thickened slightly.
Sprinkle with the chilies and cilantro
leaves and serve with steamed rice.

Serves 4

Note: Store the rest of the curry paste
in the freezer.

Caribbean fish soup

2 tomatoes
2 tablespoons vegetable oil
4 French shallots, finely chopped
2 celery stalks, chopped
1 large red pepper, chopped
1 Scotch bonnet chili, deseeded and
  finely chopped (see Note)
½ teaspoon ground allspice
½ teaspoon freshly grated nutmeg
3¾ cups fish stock
10 oz. (about 2 medium) orange
  sweet potatoes, peeled and cut
  into cubes
¼ cup lime juice
1 lb. 2 oz. skinless sea bream fillets,
  cut into chunks

Fish substitution
  sea bass, cod

Score a cross in the base of each tomato. Soak the tomatoes in boiling water for 30 seconds, then plunge into cold water. Drain and peel the skin away from the cross. Chop the tomatoes, discarding the cores and reserving any juices.

Heat the oil in a large saucepan, then add the shallots, celery, pepper, chili, allspice, and nutmeg. Cook for 4–5 minutes or until the vegetables have softened, stirring now and then. Add the chopped tomatoes (including their juices) and stock and bring to a boil. Reduce the heat to medium and add the cubes of sweet potato. Season to taste with salt and pepper and cook for about 15 minutes or until the sweet potato cubes are tender.

Add the lime juice and chunks of fish to the saucepan and poach gently for 4–5 minutes or until the fish is cooked through. Season to taste, then serve with lots of crusty bread.

Serves 6

Note: Scotch bonnet chilies look like small peppers and can be green, red, or orange. They are extremely hot but have a good, slightly acidic flavor.

Creamy cod stew

3 ripe tomatoes
1 tablespoon dried shrimp
1/4 cup vegetable oil
1 onion, chopped
1 small green pepper, chopped
1 small green chili, finely chopped
3 garlic cloves, crushed
3 tablespoons crunchy peanut butter
1 3/4 cups coconut milk
3 1/2 oz. small okra, topped and tailed
1/2 teaspoon paprika
1 lb. 5 oz. skinless cod fillet
3 tablespoons cilantro leaves

Fish substitution
  bream, bass, shrimp

Score a cross in the base of each tomato. Soak in boiling water for 30 seconds, then plunge into cold water. Drain and peel the skin away from the cross. Chop the tomatoes, discarding the cores and reserving any juices. Put the dried shrimp in a small bowl, cover with boiling water, and leave to soak for 10 minutes, then drain.

Heat the oil in a deep-sided frying pan or sauté pan. Add the onion and pepper and cook for 5 minutes, stirring occasionally. Add the chili and garlic and cook for another 2 minutes. Add the tomatoes and juices, peanut butter, coconut milk, okra, paprika, and shrimp. Bring the mixture to a boil, then reduce the heat to medium and simmer for 12–15 minutes or until the okra is tender. Meanwhile, cut the cod into large chunks.

Add the fish to the pan, stir, and simmer gently to cook. Test after 3 minutes—if the cod flakes easily, it is ready. Season to taste and sprinkle the cilantro on top.

Serves 4

Lobster curry with pepper

2 raw lobster tails (12 oz. each)
1 tablespoon vegetable oil
1–2 tablespoons red curry paste
2 stems of lemongrass, white part
  only, finely chopped
1 red pepper, roughly chopped
6 black dried Chinese dates (see
  Note)
9-oz. can coconut milk
1 tablespoon fish sauce
2 teaspoons brown sugar
1 teaspoon grated lime zest
6 tablespoons cilantro leaves,
  for garnish
lime wedges, for serving

Fish substitution
  shrimp

Cut down the sides of the lobster tails on the underside. Remove the flesh and cut it into 3/4-inch slices.

Heat the oil over medium heat in a wok or deep, heavy-based frying pan. Add the curry paste and lemongrass and stir for 1 minute. Add the lobster pieces, a few at a time, and stir-fry each batch for 2 minutes or until golden and just cooked. Remove from the wok.

Add the chopped pepper to the wok and stir-fry for 30 seconds. Add the dates and coconut milk, bring to a boil, and cook for 5 minutes or until the dates are plump. Add the fish sauce, brown sugar, and lime zest. Return the lobster to the wok and heat through for 2–3 minutes. Garnish with the cilantro leaves and serve with lime wedges and steamed jasmine rice.

Serves 4

Note: Asian markets sell dried Chinese dates, which are sometimes called jujubes.

Manhattan-style clam chowder

4 tablespoons butter
3 slices bacon, chopped
2 onions, chopped
2 garlic cloves, finely chopped
2 celery stalks, sliced
3 potatoes, diced
1 tablespoon chopped thyme
5 cups fish stock
2 lb. 4 oz. baby clams, cleaned
1 tablespoon tomato paste
14-oz. can chopped tomatoes
13 oz. skinless ling fillets, cut into
　bite-size pieces
12 large shrimp, peeled and
　deveined, tails intact
2 tablespoons chopped parsley

Fish substitution
　cod, hake, canned baby clams

Melt the butter in a large saucepan, then cook the bacon, onion, garlic, and celery over low heat, stirring occasionally, for 5 minutes or until soft but not brown. Add the potatoes, thyme, and 4 cups of the stock to the saucepan and bring to a boil. Reduce the heat and simmer, covered, for 15 minutes.

Pour the remaining stock into another saucepan and bring to a boil. Add the clams, cover, and cook for about 3–5 minutes or until they open. Discard any that do not open. Drain the clam liquid through a muslin-lined sieve and add it to the soup mixture. Pull most of the clams out of their shells, leaving a few intact for garnish.

Stir the tomato paste and chopped tomatoes into the soup and bring back to a boil. Add the fish pieces, clams, and shrimp and simmer over low heat for 3 minutes or until the seafood is cooked—the shrimp should be pink and the fish opaque. Season with salt and pepper and stir in the parsley. Serve garnished with the clams in their shells.

Serves 4

Laksa lemak

4 oz. rice noodles

Paste
3 red chilies, deseeded and chopped
2 stems of lemongrass
small knob of fresh ginger, grated
4 red Asian shallots, peeled
1 tablespoon shrimp paste
1 tablespoon ground turmeric

1/2 cup candlenuts or unsalted
  macadamias
1 tablespoon vegetable oil
2 (14-oz.) cans coconut milk
1/3 cup lime juice
4 oz. bean sprouts, trimmed
20 tiger shrimp, peeled and deveined
16 large scallops, cleaned
1/4 cup Vietnamese mint, most
  shredded, the rest left whole for
  garnish
1/2 small cucumber, peeled and
  thinly sliced

Fish substitution
  any other large shrimp, cubes of
  any firm-fleshed white fish

Soak the noodles in a bowl of boiling water for 10 minutes. Drain.

To make the paste, put all the paste ingredients, plus a tablespoon of water, into a food processor and blend until smooth. Alternatively, chop finely by hand and mix well.

Put the nuts in a saucepan and cook over medium heat until golden, then remove to a plate. Heat the oil in the same saucepan, then add the prepared paste and cook over medium heat for 2 minutes. Stir in the coconut milk, then simmer gently for 10 minutes or until it thickens slightly. Roughly chop the nuts.

When the coconut milk mixture is ready, add the lime juice and three-quarters of the bean sprouts to the pan. Season with salt, then bring back to a simmer, add the shrimp and scallops, and cook for about 5 minutes or until the shrimp turn pink. Add the shredded mint and the noodles. Mix the whole mint with the chopped nuts and cucumber.

Ladle the seafood and liquid into four deep bowls, then sprinkle with the remaining bean sprouts and top with the cucumber and nut mixture.

Serves 4

Shrimp pot pies

4 tablespoons butter
1 leek (white part only), thinly sliced
1 garlic clove, finely chopped
2 lb. 4 oz. shrimp, peeled and
 deveined, tails intact
1 tablespoon all-purpose flour
$3/4$ cup chicken or fish stock
$1/2$ cup dry white wine
2 cups cream
2 tablespoons lemon juice
1 tablespoon chopped dill
1 tablespoon chopped Italian parsley
1 teaspoon Dijon mustard
1 sheet frozen puff pastry, just thawed
1 egg, lightly beaten

Preheat the oven to 425°F. Melt the butter in a saucepan over low heat. Cook the leek and garlic for 2 minutes, then add the shrimp and cook for 1–2 minutes or until just pink. Remove the shrimp with a slotted spoon and set aside.

Stir the flour into the pan and cook for 1 minute. Add the stock and wine, bring to a boil, and cook for 10 minutes or until nearly all the liquid has evaporated. Stir in the cream, bring to a boil, then reduce the heat and simmer for 20 minutes or until the liquid reduces by half. Stir in the lemon juice, herbs, and mustard.

Using half the sauce, pour an even amount into four 1-cup ramekins. Divide the shrimp among the ramekins, then top with the remaining sauce.

Cut the pastry into four rounds, slightly larger than the rims of the ramekins. Place the pastry rounds over the shrimp mixture and press around the edges. Prick the pastry and brush with beaten egg. Bake for 20 minutes or until the pastry is crisp and golden. Serve with a salad and bread.

Serves 4

Lobster soup with zucchini and avocado

4 tablespoons butter
1 garlic clove, crushed
2 French shallots, finely chopped
1 onion, chopped
1 zucchini, diced
2½ tablespoons dry white wine
1¾ cups fish stock
9 oz. raw lobster meat, chopped
1 cup heavy cream
1 avocado, diced
1 tablespoon chopped cilantro leaves
1 tablespoon chopped parsley
lemon juice, to serve

Fish substitution
crayfish, shrimp

Melt the butter in a large saucepan. Add the garlic, shallots, onion, and zucchini. Cook over medium heat for 8–10 minutes or until the vegetables are just soft.

Splash in the wine and bring to a boil, continuing to boil for 3 minutes. Pour in the stock and bring to a boil again. Reduce the heat to low, add the chunks of lobster, and simmer for 3–4 minutes or until the lobster meat is opaque and tinged pink. Gently stir in the cream and season with salt and pepper.

Ladle the soup into four bowls and stir a little of the avocado, cilantro, and parsley into each one. Squeeze a little lemon juice over the soup before serving.

Serves 4

African fish stew

4 (7-oz.) kingfish steaks
1 large onion, sliced
1 red pepper, thinly sliced
½ cup plus 2 tablespoons
  vegetable oil
⅓ cup lemon juice
1 teaspoon cayenne pepper
½ cup fish stock

Fish substitution
  butterfish, marlin

Put the fish in a shallow, nonmetallic dish. Sprinkle the onion and red pepper on the top. Combine ⅓ cup of the oil with the lemon juice and cayenne pepper, then pour over the fish, cover, and leave to marinate for 30 minutes in the fridge.

Remove the onion and red pepper from the dish and pat dry. Heat 2 tablespoons of the remaining oil in a deep-sided frying pan, then add the onion and red pepper. Reduce the heat to low and cook gently for 10 minutes to soften, stirring now and then. Meanwhile, lift the fish out of the marinade and pat dry, reserving the marinade.

Transfer the onion and red pepper to a plate and heat the remaining oil in the pan. Sear the fish for 1 minute on each side. Return the onion and red pepper to the pan with the marinade and stock. Bring the liquid to a boil, then reduce the heat to low and cook gently, covered, for 7 minutes or until the fish is cooked through. Season to taste and serve with the onion and red pepper.

Serves 4

Mild Indian shrimp curry

4 tablespoons ghee or butter
1 onion, finely chopped
2 ripe tomatoes
2 large garlic cloves, finely chopped
1/2 teaspoon grated fresh ginger
2 small red chilies, deseeded and
  finely chopped
1 teaspoon ground coriander
1 teaspoon ground cumin
1 teaspoon garam masala
pinch of ground turmeric
2 tablespoons tomato paste
14-oz. can coconut milk
16 jumbo shrimp, peeled and
  deveined, tails intact
2 tablespoons shredded mint

Fish substitution
  chunks of firm white fish

Melt the ghee in a saucepan and, when hot, add the chopped onion. Cook for 8–10 minutes or until the onion is softened.

Meanwhile, score a cross in the base of each tomato. Put the tomatoes in boiling water for 30 seconds, then plunge into cold water. Drain, then peel the skin away from the cross. Roughly chop the tomatoes, discarding the cores and seeds and reserving any juices.

Add the garlic, ginger, and chilies to the onion and cook for 2 minutes. Stir in the spices and cook for 1 minute. Add the tomatoes and their juice, tomato paste, and coconut milk. Bring to just below boiling point and simmer for 10 minutes. Add the shrimp and cook for 3–5 minutes or until the shrimp have turned pale pink and opaque. Season with salt and stir in the mint. Serve with chapatis or naan bread to soak up the sauce, or with plain boiled basmati rice.

Serves 4

New England clam chowder

3 lb. 5 oz. clams, cleaned
2 teaspoons vegetable oil
3 slices bacon, chopped
1 onion, chopped
1 garlic clove, crushed
1 lb. 10 oz. (about 5 medium)
  potatoes, diced
1⅓ cups fish stock
2 cups milk
½ cup cream
3 tablespoons chopped Italian parsley

Put the clams in a large, heavy-based saucepan with 1 cup water, cover, and simmer for about 4 minutes or until they open. Discard any that do not open. Strain the liquid through a muslin-lined sieve and reserve. Pull most of the clams out of their shells, leaving a few intact for garnish.

Heat the oil in the cleaned saucepan. Add the bacon, onion, and garlic and cook, stirring, over medium heat until the onion is soft and the bacon is golden. Add the potatoes and stir well.

Add enough water to the reserved clam liquid to make 1⅓ cups of liquid. Pour this and the stock into the saucepan and bring to a boil, then pour in the milk and bring back to a boil. Reduce the heat, cover, and simmer for 20 minutes or until the potatoes are tender. Uncover and simmer for 10 minutes or until slightly thickened. Add the cream, clam meat, and parsley and season to taste. Heat through gently, but do not allow it to boil or it may curdle. Serve in deep bowls with the clams in shells as a garnish.

Serves 4

Bouillabaisse

Rouille
1 small red pepper
1 slice of white bread, crust removed
1 red chili
2 garlic cloves
1 egg yolk
⅓ cup olive oil

Soup
2 tablespoons vegetable oil
1 fennel bulb, thinly sliced
1 onion, chopped
1 lb. 10 oz. (about 5 medium) ripe
    tomatoes
5 cups fish stock or water
pinch of saffron threads
bouquet garni (see Note)
2-inch piece of orange zest
3 lb. 5 oz. monkfish fillets, cut into
    bite-size pieces
18 black mussels, cleaned

Fish substitution
    rascasse, sea bass, snapper, red
    mullet, John Dory, eel (skin on)

To make the rouille, preheat the broiler. Cut the pepper in half lengthwise, remove the seeds and membrane, and place, skin-side up, under the hot broiler until the skin blackens and blisters. Alternatively, hold the pepper over the gas flame of your stove until the skin is blackened. Leave to cool before peeling away the skin. Roughly chop the pepper flesh. Soak the bread in 1/4 cup water, then squeeze dry with your hands. Put the pepper, bread, chili, garlic, and egg yolk in a mortar and pestle or food processor and pound or mix together. Gradually add the olive oil in a thin stream, pounding or mixing until the rouille is smooth and has the texture of thick mayonnaise. Cover and refrigerate the rouille until needed.

Heat the vegetable oil in a large saucepan and cook the fennel and onion for 5 minutes or until golden.

Meanwhile, score a cross in the base of each tomato. Cover the tomatoes with boiling water for 30 seconds, then plunge them into cold water. Drain and peel the skin away from the cross. Chop the tomatoes, discarding the cores. Add the chopped tomato to the saucepan and cook for 3 minutes. Stir in the stock, saffron, bouquet garni, and orange zest, bring to a boil, and boil for 10 minutes. Remove the bouquet garni and orange zest and either push the soup through a sieve or puree in a blender. Return to the cleaned saucepan, season well, and bring back to a boil. Reduce the heat to a simmer and add the fish and mussels. Cook for 5 minutes or until the fish is tender and the mussels have opened. Throw away any mussels that haven't opened by this time. Serve the soup with rouille and bread or toast.

Serves 6

Note: A bouquet garni is used for flavoring soups and stews. You can buy dried ones in the supermarket (you will find them with the herbs) or make your own by wrapping the green part of a leek around a bay leaf, a sprig of thyme, a sprig of parsley, and celery leaves. Tie the bundle with kitchen string.

Fish molee

1 tablespoon vegetable oil
1 large onion, thinly sliced
3 garlic cloves, crushed
1–2 small green chilies, finely
  chopped
2 teaspoons ground turmeric
1 teaspoon ground coriander
1 teaspoon ground cumin
4 cloves
6 curry leaves, plus another 6 for
  garnish
3½ cups coconut milk
1 lb. 2 oz. skinless pomfret fillets
1 tablespoon chopped fresh cilantro
  leaves

Fish substitution
  flounder, sole, plaice, Pacific Dory

Heat the oil in a deep frying pan or sauté pan and cook the onion for 5 minutes. Add the garlic and chili and cook for another 5 minutes or until the onion has softened and looks translucent. Add the turmeric, coriander, cumin, and cloves and stir-fry with the onion for about 2 minutes before stirring in the curry leaves, coconut milk, and ½ teaspoon salt. Bring to just below boiling point. Reduce the heat to medium and simmer, without a lid, for 20 minutes or until slightly thickened.

Cut each fish fillet into two or three large pieces across the fillet. Add the fish to the sauce and bring the sauce back to a simmer, then cook for 5 minutes or until the fish is opaque and looks flaky. Season with a little more salt if necessary, then stir in the fresh cilantro. Serve garnished with curry leaves and with boiled rice to soak up the sauce.

Serves 4

Gumbo

Roux
⅓ cup vegetable oil
scant ⅔ cup all-purpose flour
1 onion, finely chopped
6 cups boiling water

4 crabs, cleaned
1 lb. chorizo sausage, cut into
    bite-size pieces
6 scallions, sliced
1 green pepper, roughly chopped
3 tablespoons chopped parsley
¼ teaspoon chili powder
1 lb. 2 oz. shrimp, peeled and
    deveined
24 oysters, shucked
½ teaspoon filé powder (see Note)
1½ tablespoons long-grain rice

To make the roux, pour the oil into a large, heavy-based saucepan over low heat. Gradually add the flour, stirring after each addition, to make a thin roux. Continue to cook and stir over low heat for 35 minutes or until it turns dark brown. Add the onion and cook for 4 minutes or until tender. Gradually pour in the boiling water, continually stirring to dissolve the roux, and bring to a simmer.

Cut the crabs into small pieces. Add the crab, sausage, scallions, pepper, parsley, and chili powder to the roux. Cook for 30 minutes, then add the shrimp and the oysters and their juices and cook for another 5 minutes or until the shrimp are pink. Season well with salt and pepper, then stir in the filé powder.

Meanwhile, cook the rice in salted boiling water for about 10 minutes or until it is just cooked through. Ladle the gumbo into bowls, each containing a couple of tablespoons of rice in the bottom.

Serves 6

Note: Filé powder is a flavoring often used in Creole cooking. It is made by drying and grinding sassafras leaves.

Fish smothered with curry sauce

⅓ cup vegetable oil
1 lb. 5 oz. skinless pomfret fillets
2 large garlic cloves, crushed
4 tablespoons red curry paste
9-oz. can coconut milk
⅓ cup fish sauce
2 tablespoons sugar
2 teaspoons lemon juice
2 teaspoons kaffir lime leaves, finely
   shredded, or 2 teaspoons lime zest
2 tablespoons chopped cilantro
   leaves, plus whole leaves for garnish

Fish substitution
   flounder, sole, plaice, cod, shrimp

Heat 2 tablespoons of the oil in a wok or sauté pan until hot. Add the fish, in batches if necessary, and cook for 2–3 minutes or until opaque. Transfer to a plate and cover with foil.

Wipe out the inside of the wok with paper towels and add the remaining oil. Heat the oil until hot, then add the garlic and curry paste and fry for 30 seconds. Pour in the coconut milk and mix. Add the fish sauce, sugar, and lemon juice and heat through. Stir in the lime leaves and chopped cilantro and spoon the curry sauce over the fish. Garnish with cilantro leaves.

Serves 4

Hearty seafood soup

2 tablespoons dried shrimp
¼ cup olive oil
1 large onion, finely chopped
3 garlic cloves, crushed
1 small red chili, deseeded and
   finely chopped
1 teaspoon finely grated fresh ginger
3 tablespoons crunchy peanut butter
28-oz. can chopped tomatoes
1¾ oz. creamed coconut, chopped
   (see Note)
14-oz. can coconut milk
generous pinch of ground cloves
¼ cup chopped cilantro leaves
1 lb. 9 oz. swordfish, cut into large
   chunks
3½ oz. small shrimp, peeled and
   deveined
2 tablespoons chopped cashews

Fish substitution
   marlin, tuna, monkfish

Soak the dried shrimp in boiling water for 10 minutes, then drain.

Heat the oil in a deep saucepan and cook the onion gently for 5 minutes. Add the garlic, chili, and ginger and cook for 2 minutes. Stir in the shrimp, peanut butter, tomatoes, creamed coconut, coconut milk, ground cloves, and half of the cilantro. Bring the mixture to a boil, reduce the heat, and simmer gently for 10 minutes.

Remove the sauce from the heat, allow to cool a little, then pour into a food processor or blender and blend until thick and smooth. Alternatively, push the mixture through a coarse sieve by hand.

Return the sauce to the pan over medium heat. Add the swordfish and cook for 2 minutes, then add the shrimp and continue to simmer until all the seafood is cooked—the shrimp will be pink and the fish opaque. Serve with the cashews and remaining cilantro sprinkled over the top.

Serves 4

Note: Creamed coconut is sold in a block. It needs to be chopped or grated and then stirred into a hot liquid. If you can't find it, use a 5-oz. can of thick coconut cream.

Mexican soup with salsa

¼ cup olive oil
1 large onion, chopped
1 large celery stalk, chopped
3 garlic cloves, crushed
2 small, thin red chilies, deseeded
   and finely chopped
scant 1 cup fish stock
28-oz. can chopped tomatoes
2 bay leaves
1 teaspoon dried oregano
1 teaspoon superfine sugar
2 large ears of corn, kernels removed
1 lb. 2 oz. halibut fillets, skinned
2 tablespoons chopped cilantro
   leaves
juice of 2 limes
12 shrimp, peeled and deveined,
   tails intact
8 scallops, cleaned
12 clams, cleaned
½ cup heavy cream

Salsa
½ small avocado
1 tablespoon cilantro leaves
finely grated zest and juice of 1 lime
½ small red onion, finely chopped

Fish substitution
   swordfish, kingfish, snapper

Heat the oil in a large saucepan. Add the onion and celery and cook over medium heat for 10 minutes, stirring now and then. Add the garlic and chili to the pan and cook for 1 minute, stirring. Add the fish stock and tomatoes and break up the tomatoes in the pan using a wooden spoon.

Stir in the bay leaves, oregano, and sugar and bring to a boil. Allow to bubble for 2 minutes, then reduce the heat to low and simmer for 10 minutes. Cool for 5 minutes, remove the bay leaves, then pour the tomato mixture into a food processor or blender and whizz until fairly smooth but not completely so. Alternatively, push the mixture through a coarse sieve by hand.

Return the tomato sauce to the saucepan and season with salt. Add the corn kernels and bring back to a boil. Reduce the heat to a simmer to cook for 3 minutes or until the kernels are just tender. Cut the fish into large chunks.

Stir the cilantro and the lime juice into the sauce, add the fish to the pan, then simmer gently for a minute. Add the shrimp and scallops and sprinkle the clams on the top. Cover with a lid and cook gently for another 2–3 minutes or until the seafood is opaque and cooked through, the shrimp have turned pink, and the clams have steamed open. Discard any clams that have not opened by now.

While the fish is poaching, make the salsa. Chop the avocado into small cubes and mix with the cilantro, the lime zest and juice, and red onion, and season with salt and pepper. Before serving, stir the cream into the soup, ladle into deep bowls, and top with salsa. Serve with sourdough bread.

Serves 4

Hot-and-sour fish stew

Spice paste
2 stems of lemongrass, white part
  only, each cut into 3 pieces
1 teaspoon ground turmeric
small knob of fresh galangal or ginger
3 small red chilies
1 large garlic clove, peeled
4 red Asian shallots, peeled
1 teaspoon shrimp paste

¼ cup vegetable oil
½ small red pepper, thinly sliced
3 tablespoons tamarind puree or
  lemon juice
1 tablespoon fish sauce
2 teaspoons brown sugar
8-oz. can sliced bamboo shoots,
  drained
1 lb. 2 oz. skinless pomfret fillets, cut
  into bite-size pieces
2 tablespoons chopped cilantro
  leaves
1 tablespoon chopped mint

Fish substitution
  lemon sole, plaice, sea bass,
  flounder, John Dory

To make the spice paste, put all the
ingredients in a food processor and
process to a paste. Alternatively,
finely chop all the ingredients and
mix together by hand.

Heat the oil in a large saucepan, then
add the paste. Cook for 10 minutes,
stirring. Add the pepper and cook for
another minute. Add 3 cups water,
the tamarind, fish sauce, sugar, and
½ teaspoon salt and bring to a boil.
Reduce the heat to low and simmer
for 5 minutes, then add the bamboo
shoots and fish pieces and poach the
fish gently for 3–4 minutes or until
opaque. Stir in the cilantro and mint
and serve with plenty of rice.

Serves 4

Creamy clam soup

4 lb. clams, cleaned
4 tablespoons butter
1 onion, chopped
1 celery stalk, chopped
1 large carrot, chopped
1 large leek, sliced into rings
9 oz. rutabaga, diced
3½–4½ cups fish stock
1 bay leaf
heaping ⅓ cup medium- or
    short-grain rice
scant 1 cup cream
3 tablespoons finely chopped
    parsley

Put the clams and 1 cup water in a large saucepan. Bring to a boil, then reduce the heat to medium and cover with a tight-fitting lid. Cook for 3–4 minutes or until the shells open. Strain into a bowl. Add enough stock to make 4 cups. Discard any clams that haven't opened by now. Remove all but eight of the clams from their shells.

Melt the butter in a clean saucepan. Add the vegetables and cook, covered, over medium heat for 10 minutes, stirring now and then. Add the stock and bay leaf, bring to a boil, then reduce the heat and simmer for 10 minutes. Add the rice, bring back to a boil, cover, and cook over medium heat for 15 minutes or until the rice and vegetables are tender. Take off the heat and stir in the clam meat. Remove the bay leaf and allow to cool for 10 minutes.

Puree the soup in a blender until smooth, then return to a clean saucepan. Stir in the cream and season to taste. Gently reheat the soup. Add the parsley and two clams in their shells to each bowl and ladle in the soup.

Serves 4

Malaysian fish curry

3–6 red chilies, roughly chopped, plus
  extra sliced chilies for garnish
1 onion, chopped
4 garlic cloves, peeled
3 stems of lemongrass, white part
  only, sliced
1½-inch piece of fresh ginger, sliced
2 teaspoons shrimp paste
¼ cup vegetable oil
1 tablespoon fish curry powder
  (see Note)
1 cup coconut milk
1 tablespoon tamarind concentrate
1 tablespoon kecap manis
1 lb. 2 oz. skinless ling fillets, cut
  into cubes
2 ripe tomatoes, chopped
1 tablespoon lemon juice

Fish substitution
  hake, coalfish

Combine the chilies, onion, garlic, lemongrass, ginger, and shrimp paste in a food processor and process until roughly chopped. Add 2 tablespoons of the oil and process until the mixture forms a smooth paste, regularly scraping down the side of the bowl with a spatula.

Heat the remaining oil in a wok or deep, heavy-based frying pan and add the paste. Cook for 3–4 minutes over low heat, stirring constantly, until very fragrant. Add the curry powder and stir for another 2 minutes. Add the coconut milk, tamarind, kecap manis, and 1 cup water to the wok. Bring to a boil, stirring occasionally, then reduce the heat and simmer for 10 minutes or until slightly thickened.

Add the fish, tomatoes, and lemon juice. Season to taste. Simmer for 5 minutes or until the fish is just cooked. Serve with rice.

Serves 4

Note: Fish curry powder is a special blend of spices that is well suited to seafood. It is available at Asian markets.

Cioppino

2 whole crabs
¼ cup olive oil
1 large onion, finely chopped
1 carrot, finely chopped
2–3 garlic cloves, crushed
1 red chili, finely chopped
14-oz. can chopped tomatoes
1 tablespoon tomato paste
1 cup red wine
2 cups fish stock
1 sprig of thyme
2 sprigs of parsley
13 oz. shrimp, peeled and deveined
2 lb. 4 oz. skinless mixed hake, snapper, or monkfish fillets, cut into bite-size pieces
12–15 mussels, cleaned
1 tablespoon chopped parsley, extra
1 tablespoon chopped basil

Pull the apron back from underneath each crab and separate the shells. Remove the feathery gills and intestines. Twist off the claws. Using a cleaver or large knife, cut the crabs into quarters. Crack the claws with either crab crackers or the back of a heavy knife.

Heat the oil in a large, heavy-based saucepan, add the onion, carrot, garlic, and chili, and stir over medium heat for about 5 minutes or until the onion is soft. Add the tomatoes, tomato paste, wine, stock, thyme, and parsley. Bring to a boil, reduce the heat, then cover and simmer for 30 minutes.

Add the crab pieces to the broth and simmer for 5 minutes, then add the shrimp and simmer for 1 minute. Add the fish pieces and mussels and simmer for another 2–3 minutes or until the fish pieces are opaque. Season well. Discard any unopened mussels. Sprinkle with parsley and basil. Serve, making sure you have plenty of napkins available.

Serves 4

Summer

Warm shrimp, arugula, and feta salad

4 scallions, chopped
4 Roma tomatoes, chopped
1 red pepper, chopped
14-oz. can chickpeas, drained
1 tablespoon chopped dill
3 tablespoons finely shredded basil
1/4 cup extra-virgin olive oil
4 tablespoons butter
2 lb. 4 oz. shrimp, peeled and
  deveined, tails intact
2 small red chilies, finely chopped
4 garlic cloves, crushed
2 tablespoons lemon juice
2 bunches arugula
5 1/2 oz. feta cheese

Put the scallions, tomatoes, pepper, chickpeas, dill, and basil in a large bowl and toss together well.

Heat the oil and butter in a large frying pan or wok, add the shrimp, and cook, stirring, over high heat for 3 minutes. Add the chilies and garlic and continue cooking for 2 minutes or until the shrimp turn pink. Remove the pan from the heat and stir in the lemon juice.

Rinse the arugula and pat dry. Arrange on a large serving platter, top with the tomato and chickpea mixture, then with the shrimp mixture. Crumble the feta cheese over the top, then serve.

Serves 6

Barbecued salmon cutlets with sweet cucumber dressing

2 small cucumbers, peeled, deseeded, and finely diced
1 red onion, finely chopped
1 red chili, finely chopped
2 tablespoons pickled ginger, shredded
2 tablespoons rice vinegar
1/2 teaspoon sesame oil
4 salmon cutlets
1 sheet toasted nori (dried seaweed), cut into thin strips

Fish substitution
ocean trout cutlets

Combine the cucumber, onion, chili, ginger, rice vinegar, and sesame oil in a bowl, cover, and leave at room temperature while you cook the salmon cutlets.

Preheat a barbecue and lightly brush the grill with oil. Cook the salmon on the barbecue for about 2 minutes on each side or until cooked as desired. Be careful not to overcook the fish or it will be dry—it should still be just pink in the center. Top the salmon with the cucumber dressing, then sprinkle with strips of toasted nori. Serve with steamed rice.

Serves 4

Barbecued fish with onions and ginger

2 lb. 4 oz. small, firm whole snapper, scaled and gutted
2 teaspoons green peppercorns, drained and finely crushed
2 teaspoons finely chopped red chilies
1 tablespoon fish sauce
¼ cup vegetable oil
2 onions, thinly sliced
1½-inch piece of fresh ginger, thinly sliced
3 garlic cloves, cut into very thin slivers
2 teaspoons sugar
4 scallions, finely shredded

Lemon and garlic sauce
¼ cup lemon juice
2 tablespoons fish sauce
1 tablespoon sugar
2 small red chilies, finely chopped
3 garlic cloves, chopped

Fish substitution
  bream, red emperor

Wash the fish and pat dry inside and out. Cut two or three diagonal slashes into the thickest part on both sides.

Mix the crushed pepper, chilies, and fish sauce to a paste and brush over the fish. Refrigerate for 20 minutes.

Meanwhile, to make the lemon and garlic sauce, stir the lemon juice, fish sauce, sugar, chilies, and garlic in a bowl until the sugar has dissolved.

Heat a barbecue until very hot and brush the grill with 1 tablespoon of oil. Cook the fish for 8 minutes on each side or until the flesh flakes easily when tested with a fork.

While the fish is cooking, heat the remaining oil in a pan and stir the onion over medium heat for a few minutes or until golden. Add the ginger, garlic, and sugar and cook for another 3 minutes. Serve over the fish. Sprinkle with scallions and serve with the sauce and steamed rice to soak up the sauce.

Serves 4

Herbed lobsters with sweet cider sauce

16 slipper lobsters
1/3 cup olive oil
1/2 cup plus 2 tablespoons lemon juice
3 garlic cloves, crushed
1/2 cup finely chopped Italian parsley
3 tablespoons finely chopped dill,
    plus some extra for garnish
1/3 cup apple cider
3 tablespoons butter
crusty bread, for serving
mixed salad, for serving

Fish substitution
    jumbo shrimp

Remove the heads from the lobsters, then cut them in half lengthwise. Place in a single layer in a shallow, nonmetallic dish. Combine the olive oil, lemon juice, garlic, parsley, and dill and pour over the lobsters. Cover and refrigerate for at least 1 hour.

Cook the lobsters in a large pan or on a barbecue, shell-side down, for 2 minutes. Turn and cook for another 2 minutes or until tender. Transfer to a serving platter.

Simmer the apple cider in a small saucepan until reduced by two-thirds. Reduce the heat and add the butter, stirring until melted. Remove from the heat, pour over the lobster, and serve. Serve with crusty bread and a green salad.

Serves 4

Note: Slipper lobsters may be expensive, so replace with an equivalent amount of small or spiny lobster tails if cost is an issue.

Swordfish shish kebabs with herb yogurt and couscous

1 lb. 12 oz. skinless swordfish fillet,
   cut into 1¼-inch chunks
⅓ cup lemon juice
⅓ cup olive oil
3 bay leaves
16 whole cherry tomatoes or 2 firm
   tomatoes, each cut into 8 wedges
2 small red onions, each cut into
   8 wedges
2 small red or orange peppers, each
   deseeded and cut into 8 chunks

Lemon and herb yogurt
scant 1 cup yogurt
1 tablespoon lemon juice
pinch of paprika
1 tablespoon finely chopped mint
1 tablespoon finely chopped parsley

Couscous
2 cups instant couscous
1¾ cups hot stock
1 tablespoon olive oil
2 tablespoons butter

Fish substitution
   tuna, marlin, kingfish, barramundi

Put the chunks of swordfish in a nonmetallic bowl with the lemon juice, olive oil, and bay leaves. Toss to mix, cover, and leave to marinate for at least 2 hours in the fridge.

In a small bowl, whisk together the ingredients for the lemon and herb yogurt. Refrigerate until needed.

Thread five chunks of fish, two cherry tomatoes, two pieces of onion, and two pieces of pepper onto a metal skewer, alternating between the fish and the various vegetables as you go. You'll need eight skewers in total.

Cook the kebabs on a grill pan or barbecue for 8–10 minutes. Baste with the remaining marinade as they cook, and turn every now and then. When ready, the fish should be firm and opaque and the vegetables slightly charred.

Meanwhile, put the couscous into a heatproof bowl, add the stock and oil, cover tightly, and leave to sit for 5 minutes. Fluff the grains with a fork and stir in the butter.

Serve the kebabs on a mound of couscous, drizzled with some of the yogurt dressing.

Serves 4

Caesar salad with sardines

Dressing
1 egg
2 garlic cloves
2 tablespoons lemon juice
½ teaspoon Worcestershire sauce
3–4 anchovy fillets
½ cup extra-virgin olive oil

1 cup dry bread crumbs
⅔ cup grated Parmesan cheese
2 tablespoons chopped fresh parsley
2 eggs, lightly beaten
⅓ cup milk
16 sardines, scaled and split down
 the middle
vegetable oil, for deep-frying
12 small pappadams
1 baby cos lettuce, leaves separated
8 slices of prosciutto, cooked
 until crisp
½ cup shaved Parmesan cheese

Fish substitution
 small herring, mackerel

To make the dressing, put the egg in a food processor, add the garlic, lemon juice, Worcestershire sauce, and anchovies, and process to combine. With the motor running, add the oil in a thin, steady stream until the dressing has thickened slightly. Refrigerate until you're ready to serve.

Put the bread crumbs, grated Parmesan, and parsley in a bowl and mix well. Put the beaten eggs and milk in another bowl and whisk well. Dip the sardines into the egg mixture, then into the crumb mixture, and put on a baking tray lined with waxed paper. Refrigerate for an hour.

Heat the oil in a deep-fat fryer or heavy-based frying pan until it reaches 350°F or until a small cube of white bread dropped into the oil browns in 15 seconds. Deep-fry the pappadams until crisp, then drain on paper towels. Deep-fry the sardines in batches until crisp and golden.

Arrange the lettuce on a plate, top with the prosciutto, sardines, pappadams, and shaved Parmesan, then drizzle with the dressing.

Serves 4

Cajun swordfish

1 tablespoon garlic powder
1 tablespoon onion powder
2 teaspoons white pepper
2 teaspoons cracked black pepper
2 teaspoons dried thyme
2 teaspoons dried oregano
1 teaspoon cayenne pepper
4 swordfish steaks
vegetable oil, for cooking
lime wedges, for serving
plain yogurt, for serving
mixed salad leaves, for serving

Fish substitution
  tuna, mahimahi, kingfish,
  striped marlin

Mix all the dried spices and herbs in a bowl. Pat the swordfish steaks dry with paper towels, then coat both sides of each steak in the spice mixture, shaking off any excess.

Heat a barbecue and brush the grill with a little oil. Cook the swordfish steaks for 3–5 minutes on each side, depending on the thickness of each steak. Serve with wedges of lime, a dollop of yogurt, and a salad.

Serves 4

Rosemary tuna kebabs

3 tomatoes
1 tablespoon olive oil
2–3 small red chilies, deseeded
and chopped
3–4 garlic cloves, crushed
1 red onion, finely chopped
¼ cup white wine or water
14-oz. can chickpeas, drained
3 tablespoons chopped oregano
4 tablespoons chopped parsley
lemon wedges, for serving

Tuna kebabs
2 lb. 4 oz. tuna, cut into 1½-inch
cubes
8 stems of rosemary, about 8 inches
long, with the leaves from the stem
thinned out a little
vegetable oil spray

Fish substitution
swordfish, striped marlin, salmon

Cut the tomatoes into halves or quarters and use a spoon to scrape out the seeds. Roughly chop the flesh.

Heat the oil in a large, nonstick frying pan. Add the chili, garlic, and red onion and stir over medium heat for 5 minutes or until softened. Add the chopped tomatoes and the white wine or water. Cook over low heat for 10 minutes or until the mixture is soft and pulpy and most of the liquid has evaporated. Stir in the chickpeas with the oregano and parsley. Season to taste with salt and freshly ground black pepper.

Heat a broiler or barbecue. Thread the tuna onto the rosemary stems, lightly spray with oil, then cook, turning, for 3 minutes or until lightly browned on the outside but still a little pink in the center. Serve with the tomato and chickpea mixture and some lemon wedges.

Serves 4

Redfish in corn husks with asparagus and red pepper dressing

Red pepper dressing
1 red pepper
2 tablespoons virgin olive oil
1 small garlic clove, crushed
1 tablespoon lemon juice
1 tablespoon chopped basil
1 tablespoon pine nuts
1/2 cup small black olives

6 small redfish, scaled and gutted
12 sprigs of lemon thyme
1 lemon, sliced
2 garlic cloves, sliced
12 large corn husks
olive oil, for drizzling
2 bunches of fresh asparagus, trimmed
lemon wedges, for serving

To make the dressing, cut the pepper into large pieces. Put skin-side up under a hot broiler until the skin blackens and blisters. Alternatively, hold over the coals or gas flame of a barbecue. Cool in a plastic bag, then peel off the skin. Finely dice the flesh.

Combine the olive oil, garlic, lemon juice, and basil in a small bowl and whisk together. Add the pepper, pine nuts, and olives.

Wash the fish and pat dry inside and out with paper towels. Fill each fish cavity with thyme, lemon, and garlic, then place each in a corn husk. Drizzle with oil and sprinkle with black pepper, then top each fish with another husk. Tie each end of the husks with string to enclose.

Place on a barbecue and cook, turning once, for 6–8 minutes or until the fish is cooked and flakes easily when tested with a fork. A few minutes after you've started cooking the fish, brush the asparagus with oil and cook, turning occasionally, on the barbecue for 3–4 minutes or until tender. Pour the dressing over the asparagus and serve with the fish and lemon wedges.

Serves 6

Lemon and herb rainbow trout

3 tablespoons chopped dill
2 tablespoons chopped rosemary
4 tablespoons roughly chopped
    Italian parsley
2 teaspoons thyme
1½ tablespoons green peppercorns,
    drained and crushed
⅓ cup lemon juice
1 lemon, sliced, plus some extra
    slices for garnish (optional)
4 whole rainbow trout, scaled and
    gutted
⅓ cup dry white wine

Horseradish cream
1 tablespoon horseradish cream
½ cup sour cream
2 tablespoons cream

Lemon sauce
¾ cup butter
2 egg yolks
3–4 tablespoons lemon juice

Fish substitution
    baby salmon, Atlantic salmon
    steaks (see Note)

Cut eight sheets of foil large enough to wrap the fish in. Lay four of them out on a flat surface, then put a second sheet on each piece so that each piece is a double thickness. Lightly grease the top sheets.

Heat a barbecue. In a bowl, mix the herbs, crushed peppercorns, and lemon juice and add salt and freshly ground black pepper to taste. Put a few slices of lemon in each fish cavity. Wipe any slime off the fish with paper towels. Spoon the herb mixture into the fish cavities. Lay each fish on a piece of foil and sprinkle each with 1 tablespoon of wine. Fold the foil to form parcels. Cook on the barbecue for about 15 minutes or until the fish is just cooked through. If you like, cook some extra lemon slices on the barbecue to use as a garnish.

Removed the wrapped fish from the heat and let sit for 5 minutes, then serve with horseradish cream and lemon sauce.

For the horseradish cream, mix the creams in a bowl and season with salt and pepper to taste.

For the lemon sauce, melt the butter in a small saucepan over low heat, without stirring. Skim the foam off the surface and pour off the clear yellow liquid, leaving the milky sediment behind. Discard the sediment. Blend the egg yolks in a food processor for 20 seconds. With the motor running, add the clear yellow butter slowly in a thin, steady stream. Continue processing until all the butter has been added and the mixture is thick and creamy. Add the lemon juice and season with salt and pepper. Garnish the fish with barbecued lemon slices and some strips of chives if you like.

Serves 4

Note: If you are using Atlantic salmon steaks, place the salmon on a bed of the lemon slices and spread the herb mixture over the top, or cut a slit through the center of the steak and fill with the lemon and herb mixture.

Smoked tuna and white bean salad with basil dressing

2 handfuls arugula
1 small red pepper, julienned
1 small red onion, chopped
11-oz. can cannellini beans, drained
  and rinsed
4 1/2 oz. cherry tomatoes, cut into
  halves
2 tablespoons capers, rinsed and
  squeezed dry
2 (4 1/2-oz.) cans smoked tuna slices
  in oil, drained

Basil dressing
1 tablespoon lemon juice
1 tablespoon white wine
1/4 cup extra-virgin olive oil
1 garlic clove, crushed
2 tablespoons chopped basil
1/2 teaspoon sugar

fish substitution
  fresh tuna, seared on both sides,
  then sliced, or canned salmon or
  tuna

Trim any long stems from the arugula, rinse, pat dry, and divide among four serving plates.

Lightly toss the pepper in a large bowl with the onion, beans, tomatoes, and capers. Spoon some onto each plate, over the arugula, then sprinkle tuna on top.

For the dressing, thoroughly whisk all the ingredients in a bowl with 1 tablespoon water, 1/4 teaspoon salt, and freshly ground black pepper to taste. Drizzle over the salad and serve with bread.

Serves 4

Fish tikka

Marinade
2 cups plain yogurt
2 red Asian shallots, finely chopped
1 tablespoon grated fresh ginger
2 garlic cloves, crushed
2 tablespoons lemon juice
1 teaspoon ground coriander
1 tablespoon garam masala
1 teaspoon paprika
1 teaspoon chili powder
2 tablespoons tomato paste

1 lb. 2 oz. skinless shark
2 onions, each cut into 8 chunks
2 small green or red peppers, each
 deseeded and cut into 8 chunks
1 small cucumber, peeled and diced
2 tablespoons chopped cilantro
 leaves
lemon wedges, for serving

Fish substitution
 sea bream, snapper, grouper,
 orange roughy, sea bass

To make the marinade, mix half of the yogurt, all of the other marinade ingredients, and 1 teaspoon salt together in a shallow, nonmetallic dish that is long enough and deep enough to hold eight metal skewers.

Cut the fish into approximately twenty-four bite-size pieces. On each skewer, thread three pieces of fish and two chunks each of onion and pepper, alternating them as you go. Turn the skewers in the dish containing the marinade so that all the fish and vegetables are well coated. Cover and leave to marinate for at least an hour in the fridge.

Preheat the barbecue or broiler. Lift the skewers out of the marinade. Cook them on the barbecue or under the broiler for about 5 minutes or until the fish is firm and opaque.

Meanwhile, stir the cucumber and cilantro into the remaining yogurt. Serve the fish with the yogurt and lemon wedges.

Serves 4

Barbecued calamari with picada dressing

1 lb. 10 oz. small calamari, cleaned
arugula leaves, for serving
crusty bread, for serving

Picada dressing
¼ cup extra-virgin olive oil
3 tablespoons finely chopped Italian
  parsley
2 garlic cloves, crushed

fish substitution
  cuttlefish, octopus, shrimp, or even
  chunks of firm white fish fillet

To clean the calamari, gently pull the tentacles away from the tube (the intestines should come away at the same time). Remove the intestines from the tentacles by cutting under the eyes, then remove the beak (if it remains in the center of the tentacles) by using your fingers to push up the center. Pull away the soft bone. Rub the tubes under cold running water and the skin should come away easily. Wash the tubes and tentacles and drain well. Place in a bowl, add ¼ teaspoon salt, and mix well. Cover and refrigerate for about 30 minutes. Heat a lightly oiled flat barbecue plate.

For the picada dressing, whisk together the olive oil, parsley, garlic, ½ teaspoon freshly ground black pepper, and some salt in a small bowl.

Cook the calamari in small batches on the barbecue for about 2–3 minutes or until the tubes are white and tender. Barbecue the tentacles, turning to brown them all over, for 1 minute or until they curl up. Serve hot, drizzled with the picada dressing, with arugula leaves and crusty bread.

Serves 4

Salade Niçoise

3 large eggs
1 1/2 cups green beans, trimmed and
    cut in half

Dressing
1/2 cup olive oil
1/4 cup red wine vinegar
1 teaspoon Dijon mustard
generous pinch of sugar
1 small garlic clove, crushed

1 small cucumber, peeled and cut
    into chunks
3 ripe Roma tomatoes, each cut
    into 8 wedges
1 small red onion, thinly sliced
8 oz. crisp lettuce, torn into bite-
    size pieces
1 small red pepper, thinly sliced
6 anchovy fillets in oil, drained and
    cut in half lengthwise
10 small black olives, pitted and
    cut in half lengthwise
1–2 tablespoons torn basil
6-oz. can of tuna, preferably in
    olive oil

Fish substitution
    salmon, swordfish, marlin

Put the eggs in a saucepan of cold water and bring to a boil. Reduce the heat and simmer for 6–7 minutes. Cool the hard-boiled eggs under cold running water, peel, and cut each egg into four lengthwise.

Bring a saucepan of water to a boil and add the beans. Blanch for a minute, then drain and rinse under cold running water.

Make the dressing by whisking all the dressing ingredients together.

Combine the beans, cucumber, tomatoes, onion, lettuce, red pepper, anchovy fillets, and olives in a large bowl. Toss together to mix. Add the basil and the tuna, breaking it into large lumps, then add the dressing and gently toss again. Arrange the eggs on the salad and serve with a baguette.

Serves 4

Barbecued Asian-style seafood

1 lb. 2 oz. shrimp, peeled and
  deveined, tails intact
10½ oz. scallop meat
1 lb. 2 oz. baby calamari, cleaned,
  tubes cut into quarters
1 lb. 2 oz. baby octopus, cleaned
1 cup sweet chili sauce
1 tablespoon fish sauce
2 tablespoons lime juice
¼ cup peanut oil
lime wedges, for serving

Put the shrimp, scallops, calamari,
and octopus in a shallow, nonmetallic
bowl. In a separate bowl, combine
the sweet chili sauce, fish sauce, lime
juice, and 1 tablespoon of the peanut
oil. Pour the mixture over the seafood
and mix gently to coat. Allow to
marinate for an hour. Drain the seafood
well and reserve the marinade.

Heat the remaining oil on a flat
barbecue plate. Cook the seafood,
in batches if necessary, over high
heat for 3–5 minutes or until tender.
Drizzle each batch with a little of the
leftover marinade during cooking.
Serve on a bed of steamed rice with
lime wedges.

Serves 6

Sweet-and-sour
fish kebabs

1 lb. 10 oz. thick ling fillets
8-oz. can pineapple pieces
1 large red pepper
1 tablespoon soy sauce
1½ tablespoons brown sugar
2 tablespoons white wine vinegar
2 tablespoons tomato sauce

Fish substitution
cod, striped marlin

Soak twelve wooden skewers in cold water for 30 minutes to ensure that they don't burn during cooking. Meanwhile, cut the fish into 1-inch cubes. Drain the pineapple, reserving 2 tablespoons of liquid. Cut the pepper into 1-inch pieces. Thread the pepper, fish, and pineapple alternately onto the skewers.

Place the kebabs in a shallow, nonmetallic dish. Combine the soy sauce, reserved pineapple juice, sugar, vinegar, and tomato sauce in a small bowl. Mix well and pour over the kebabs. Cover and refrigerate for 2–3 hours.

Preheat a barbecue or grill pan and grease lightly. Cook the kebabs on the barbecue, brushing frequently with the marinade, for 2–3 minutes each side or until just cooked through. Serve immediately with a green salad.

Makes 12 skewers

Honey and lime shrimp kebabs with salsa

32 shrimp, peeled and deveined, tails intact
3 tablespoons honey
1 small red chili, deseeded and finely chopped
2 tablespoons olive oil
zest and juice of 2 limes
1 large garlic clove, crushed
3/4-inch piece of fresh ginger, finely grated
1 tablespoon chopped cilantro leaves

Salsa
2 tomatoes
1 small, just-ripe mango, diced
1/2 small red onion, diced
1 small red chili, deseeded and finely chopped
zest and juice of 1 lime
2 tablespoons chopped cilantro leaves

Put the shrimp in a nonmetallic dish. Whisk the honey, chili, olive oil, lime zest and juice, garlic, ginger, and cilantro together, then pour over the shrimp. Toss well. Cover and marinate in the fridge for at least 3 hours, turning occasionally. Meanwhile, soak eight bamboo skewers in water for 30 minutes to ensure that they don't burn during cooking.

For the salsa, score a cross in the base of each tomato. Cover with boiling water for 30 seconds, then plunge into cold water. Peel the skin away from the cross. Dice the tomatoes, discarding the cores and saving any juice. In a bowl, mix the tomatoes and their juice with the mango, red onion, chili, lime zest and juice, and cilantro.

Preheat the broiler or a barbecue to high. Thread four shrimp onto each skewer. Cook for 4 minutes, turning halfway through cooking. Baste regularly with the leftover marinade as they cook. The shrimp will turn pink and be lightly browned on both sides. Serve the kebabs with the salsa and some rice.

Serves 4

Grilled red mullet with herb sauce

4 (7-oz.) red mullets
¼ cup lemon juice
¼ cup olive oil
parsley, for garnish
lemon wedges, for serving

Herb sauce
3½ oz. spinach
¼ cup olive oil
1 tablespoon white wine vinegar
1 tablespoon chopped parsley
1 tablespoon chopped chives
1 tablespoon chopped chervil
1 tablespoon finely chopped capers
2 anchovy fillets, finely chopped
1 hard-boiled egg, finely chopped

Preheat a griddle or barbecue. Make a couple of deep slashes in the thickest part of each fish. Pat the fish dry and sprinkle inside and out with salt and pepper. Drizzle with a little lemon juice and olive oil and cook on the griddle or barbecue for 4–5 minutes each side or until the fish flakes when tested with the tip of a knife. Baste with the lemon juice and oil during cooking.

To make the sauce, wash the spinach and put it in a large saucepan with just the water clinging to the leaves. Cover the pan and steam the spinach for 2 minutes or until just wilted. Drain, cool, and squeeze with your hands to get rid of the excess liquid. Finely chop. Mix with the oil, vinegar, herbs, capers, anchovies, and egg in a food processor or mortar and pestle. Spoon the sauce onto a plate and place the fish on top. Garnish with parsley and lemon wedges.

Serves 4

Barbecued sardines with pesto

12 sardines, scaled and split open
1 cup olive oil
1 tablespoon chopped rosemary
1 tablespoon chopped thyme
1 lb. 9 oz. butternut squash
2 small red onions

Pesto
1½ cups Italian parsley
2 garlic cloves, peeled
¼ cup macadamias
scant 1 cup grated Parmesan cheese
1 cup plus 2 tablespoons olive oil

Fish substitution
gar, whiting, mackerel

Pat the sardines dry and place in a nonmetallic container. Season the fish on both sides with salt and pepper. Mix the oil with the rosemary and thyme and drizzle over the fish. Leave to marinate for an hour or until you are ready to cook. Heat a flat barbecue plate.

Meanwhile, slice the butternut squash and cut into chunks measuring about 2½ x 2 x ½ inch. Slice the onions in half widthwise.

Make the pesto by putting all the ingredients in a food processor and whizzing to a paste. Alternatively, finely chop all the ingredients by hand and mix. Season to taste.

Barbecue the squash, onion, and fish for 2–3 minutes on each side, brushing regularly with the remaining herb oil. You will need a spatula to turn the squash on the barbecue. Serve each person three sardines on a small bed of squash slices with half a red onion and a generous spoonful of pesto on the side.

Serves 4

Octopus salad

1 lb. 7 oz. baby octopus, cleaned
4 cups mixed salad leaves
lemon wedges, for serving

Dressing
2 tablespoons lemon juice
1/2 cup olive oil
1 garlic clove, thinly sliced
1 tablespoon chopped mint
1 tablespoon chopped parsley
1 teaspoon Dijon mustard
pinch of cayenne pepper

Bring a large pan of water to a boil and add the octopus. Simmer for about 8–10 minutes or until the octopuses are tender, testing with the point of a knife.

Meanwhile, make the dressing by mixing together the lemon juice, olive oil, garlic, mint, parsley, mustard, and cayenne pepper with some salt and freshly ground black pepper.

Drain the octopuses well and put in a bowl. Pour most of the dressing over the top and cool for a few minutes before transferring to the fridge. Chill for at least 3 hours before serving on a bed of salad leaves. Drizzle the remaining dressing on top and serve with lemon wedges.

Serves 4

Beer-battered fish with crunchy potato wedges

Batter
1¼ cups all-purpose flour
1½ cups beer

4 floury potatoes (such as russet),
    cut into ½-inch-wide wedges
vegetable oil, for deep-frying
4 skinless firm white fish fillets (such
    as cod or haddock), patted dry
cornstarch, for coating
lemon wedges, for serving

Fish substitution
    bream, coalfish, shark, flathead,
    pollack, snapper

Sift the flour into a large bowl and make a well in the center. Gradually pour in the beer, whisking to make a smooth batter. Cover and set aside.

Soak the potatoes in cold water for 10 minutes. Drain and pat dry. Fill a deep-fat fryer or large saucepan one-third full of oil and heat to 315°F or until a small cube of white bread browns in 30 seconds. Cook batches of potato wedges for 4–5 minutes or until lightly golden. Remove with a slotted spoon and drain on crumpled paper towels.

Dust the fish with cornstarch, dip into the batter, and shake off any excess. Deep-fry in batches for 5–7 minutes or until golden and the fish is cooked through. Turn with tongs if necessary. You can check that the fish is cooked by cutting into the center of one of the pieces—the flesh should be moist and opaque. When cooked, drain the fish on crumpled paper towels. Keep warm in a 200°F oven while you cook the potato wedges again. Reheat the oil to 350°F or until a cube of white bread browns in 15 seconds. Cook the wedges for 1–2 minutes, in batches, until crisp and golden. Drain on crumpled paper towels. Serve the fish with lemon wedges and the crunchy potato wedges.

Serves 4

Seafood pizza

Pizza dough
5 cups all-purpose flour, plus a little
  extra for dusting
1 teaspoon dried yeast or ⅛ oz.
  fresh yeast
1 tablespoon olive oil, plus a little
  extra

2 medium ripe tomatoes
2 tablespoons olive oil
1 large garlic clove, crushed
½ teaspoon sugar
pinch of chili powder
1 tablespoon tomato paste
1¾ oz. calamari, cleaned, cut into
  rings
5¾ oz. skinless cod fillets, cut into
  small chunks
4 oz. shrimp, peeled and deveined
1¾ oz. mussels, cooked, shells
  removed
8 anchovy fillets in oil, drained and
  patted dry
5½ oz. mozzarella or Gruyère cheese,
  cut into small cubes
few sprigs of basil

Fish substitution
  haddock, sole

Mix 2 teaspoons of the flour in a large bowl with ¼ cup lukewarm water. Sprinkle the yeast over the top and stir to dissolve. Leave in a draft-free spot to activate. If the mixture does not bubble and foam in 5 minutes, throw it away and start again.

Put the remaining flour, the yeast mixture, 2 teaspoons salt, the olive oil, and about 1 cup water in a large bowl or in a food mixer with a dough hook. Mix together to form a dough, turn out onto a floured surface, and knead for about 5 minutes. Put the dough back in the bowl and use your hands to smear the surface of the dough with a little extra oil to prevent it from drying out. Cover with a towel and leave in a draft-free spot for about 2 hours or until doubled in size.

Knock back the dough by punching it with your fist, then remove the dough from the bowl and divide into four portions. Dust with a little flour and roll into small balls. Place the balls on a tray or board dusted with a little flour and cover with a clean towel. Leave to rest for at least 30 minutes and up to 2 hours.

Meanwhile, make the topping for the pizza. Score a cross in the base of each tomato. Put in boiling water for 30 seconds, then plunge into cold water and peel the skin away from the cross. Roughly chop the tomatoes, discarding the cores. Heat the olive oil in a saucepan and, when hot, add the garlic. Cook for 30 seconds before adding the tomatoes, sugar, chili powder, and tomato paste. Bring the mixture to a boil, then lower to a simmer and cook, uncovered, for 20 minutes, by which time the sauce will be reduced and thick. Season.

Once the dough is ready, preheat the oven to 450°F. Heavily dust the work surface with flour to prevent the dough from sticking, then use your hands to flatten out a dough ball into a circle. Finish off with a rolling pin to make a thin crust, about ⅛ inch thick, and transfer to a baking sheet or pizza tray. Repeat with the remaining balls of dough.

Working quickly, spread the tomato mixture over the dough and sprinkle the seafood on top. Dot the cubes of cheese and sprigs of basil in between the fish. Season and bake for about 10 minutes or until the crust is golden and crisp and the topping is cooked.

Makes 4 individual pizzas

Note: If you prefer, you can use ready-made pizza crusts.

One-dish
fish

Spaghetti vongole

2 tablespoons olive oil
3 garlic cloves, crushed
2 pinches of chili flakes
½ cup dry white wine
14-oz. can chopped tomatoes
3 tablespoons finely chopped Italian
  parsley
2 lb. 4 oz. clams, cleaned
14 oz. spaghetti or linguine
½ teaspoon grated lemon zest
lemon wedges, for serving

Heat the oil in a large, deep frying pan. Add the garlic and chili and cook over low heat for 30 seconds. Add the white wine, tomatoes, and 1 teaspoon of the parsley. Increase the heat and boil, stirring occasionally, for 8–10 minutes or until the liquid is reduced by half.

Add the clams to the pan and cover with a lid. Increase the heat and cook for 3–5 minutes or until the clams open, shaking the pan often. Remove the clams from the pan, discarding any that stay closed. Stir in the remaining parsley and season. Boil the sauce for 3–4 minutes, until it is thick. Set half the clams aside and extract the meat from the rest.

Cook the pasta in a large saucepan of boiling, salted water until al dente. Drain, then stir the sauce through the pasta. Add the lemon zest, reserved clams, and clam meat and toss well. Serve with the lemon wedges.

Serves 4

Shrimp ravioli with basil butter

1 lb. 2 oz. shrimp, peeled and
   deveined
1 tablespoon chopped chives
1 egg white, lightly beaten
1 1/3 cups cream
7-oz. packet gow gee wrappers
   (see Note)
1 egg, lightly beaten

Basil butter
1/2 cup butter
1 garlic clove, crushed
3 tablespoons finely shredded basil
1/4 cup pine nuts

Put the shrimp in a food processor
with the chives and egg white and
process until smooth. Season with
salt and pepper, then add the
cream and blend, being careful not
to overprocess or the mixture will
curdle. Transfer to a bowl, cover,
and chill for 30 minutes.

Put 2–3 teaspoons of the shrimp
mixture in the center of each gow gee
wrapper (you won't need them all).
Brush the edges with beaten egg,
then fold over to form semicircles;
press the edges to seal. Add in
batches to a large pan of boiling
water and cook each batch for
4 minutes. Drain, taking care not
to damage the ravioli, and divide
among warm serving plates.

For the basil butter, melt the butter
gently in a pan, add the garlic, and
stir until fragrant. Add the basil, pine
nuts, and a little freshly ground black
pepper and cook until the butter turns
a nutty brown color. Drizzle the butter
over the ravioli. Serve immediately.

Serves 8

Note: You can find gow gee wrappers
at Asian markets—they are thin,
round wrappers made from wheat
flour and water.

Seafood risotto

7 cups fish stock
2 tablespoons olive oil
2 onions, finely chopped
2 garlic cloves, finely chopped
1 celery stalk, finely chopped
2 cups risotto rice
8–10 black mussels, cleaned
5½ oz. cod fillet, cubed
8 shrimp, peeled and deveined,
   tails intact
2 tablespoons chopped parsley
1 tablespoon chopped oregano
1 tablespoon chopped thyme

Fish substitution
   coalfish, ling

Pour the stock into a saucepan and bring to a boil. Reduce the heat until just simmering, then cover.

Heat the olive oil in a large saucepan over medium heat. Add the onion, garlic, and celery and cook for 2–3 minutes. Add 2 tablespoons water, cover with a lid, and cook for 5 minutes or until the vegetables soften. Add the rice and cook, stirring, over medium heat for 3–4 minutes or until the rice grains are well coated.

Gradually add ½ cup of the hot stock to the rice, stirring over low heat with a wooden spoon, until all the stock has been absorbed. Repeat, adding ½ cup stock each time until only a small amount of stock is left and the rice is just tender—this should take about 20–25 minutes.

Meanwhile, bring ¼ cup water to a boil in a saucepan. Add the mussels, cover with a lid, and cook for about 4–5 minutes, shaking the pan occasionally, until the mussels have opened. Drain the mussels and discard any unopened ones. Set the mussels aside until you're ready to add them to the risotto. Add the fish, shrimp, and the remaining hot stock to the rice and stir well. Cook for 5–10 minutes or until the seafood is just cooked and the rice is tender and creamy. Remove from the heat, add the mussels, cover, and set aside for 5 minutes. Stir the parsley, oregano, and thyme into the risotto, then season to taste with salt and freshly ground black pepper. Leave to cool for a couple of minutes, then serve.

Serves 4

Tagliatelle with shrimp and cream

1 lb. 2 oz. fresh tagliatelle or other
   long, flat pasta
4 tablespoons butter
6 scallions, finely chopped
1 lb. 2 oz. shrimp, peeled and
   deveined, tails intact
1/4 cup brandy
1 1/4 cups heavy cream
1 tablespoon chopped thyme
1/2 cup chopped Italian parsley

Cook the pasta in a large saucepan of boiling water until al dente. Drain well.

Meanwhile, melt the butter in a large, heavy-based pan, add the scallions, and stir for 2 minutes over medium heat. Add the shrimp and stir for 2 minutes or until they just start to change color. Remove the shrimp from the pan and set aside.

Pour the brandy into the pan and boil for 2 minutes or until the brandy is reduced by half. Stir in the cream, then add the thyme and half the parsley. Season with freshly ground black pepper. Simmer for 5 minutes or until the sauce begins to thicken. Return the shrimp to the sauce and cook for 2 minutes. Season well.

Toss the sauce through the pasta. If you prefer a thinner sauce, add a little hot water or milk. Sprinkle with the remaining parsley, then serve.

Serves 4

Seafood lasagna

1 tablespoon olive oil
2 tablespoons butter
1 onion, finely chopped
2 garlic cloves, crushed
14 oz. shrimp, peeled and deveined
1 lb. 2 oz. skinless firm white fish
   fillets, cut into $3/4$-inch pieces
9 oz. scallops with roe, cleaned
26-oz. jar tomato pasta sauce
1 tablespoon tomato paste
1 teaspoon brown sugar
$1/2$ cup grated cheddar cheese
$1/4$ cup grated Parmesan cheese
9 oz. fresh lasagna noodles

Cheese sauce
$1/2$ cup butter
$2/3$ cup all-purpose flour
6 cups milk
2 cups grated cheddar cheese
1 cup grated Parmesan cheese

Fish substitution
   hake, snapper, ling

Preheat the oven to 350°F. Lightly grease a 10¾ x 8½-inch, 10-cup ovenproof dish.

Heat the oil and butter in a large saucepan. Add the onion and cook for 2–3 minutes or until softened but not browned. Add the garlic and cook for 30 seconds or until fragrant. Add the shrimp and fish pieces and cook for 2 minutes. Add the scallops and cook for another minute. Stir in the pasta sauce, tomato paste, and sugar and simmer for 5 minutes.

Combine the ½ cup cheddar and ¼ cup Parmesan cheese in a bowl and set aside until needed for topping the lasagna.

For the cheese sauce, melt the butter over low heat in a saucepan, then stir in the flour and cook for 1 minute or until the mixture is pale and foaming. Remove the pan from the heat and gradually stir in the milk. Return the pan to the heat and stir until the sauce boils and thickens. Reduce the heat, simmer for 2 minutes, then stir in the 2 cups cheddar and 1 cup Parmesan. Season to taste with salt and freshly ground black pepper.

Line the ovenproof dish with a layer of lasagna noodles. Spoon a third of the seafood sauce into the dish over the noodles. Top with a third of the cheese sauce. Arrange another layer of noodles over the top. Repeat with the seafood sauce, cheese sauce, and lasagna noodles until you have three layers, ending with a layer of cheese sauce. Sprinkle the top with the combined cheddar and Parmesan. Bake for 30 minutes or until the top is golden. Remove from the oven and let sit for 10 minutes to firm up before slicing. Serve with a salad.

Serves 6

273

Mud crabs with rice noodles

3 lb. 5 oz. live mud crabs, each
  weighing approximately 9 oz.
5½ oz. dried thin rice noodles
5–6 tablespoons vegetable oil
2 red Asian shallots, thinly sliced
1 garlic clove, finely chopped
2 small red chilies, finely chopped
6 oz. bean sprouts, trimmed
6 oz. Chinese barbecued pork
  (char siu) or other cooked pork,
  cut into small pieces
¼ cup light soy sauce
2 tablespoons oyster sauce
2 tablespoons chopped cilantro
  leaves

Freeze the crabs for 1 hour to immobilize them. Plunge them into boiling water for 2 minutes, then drain. Wash well with a stiff brush, then pat dry. Pull the aprons back from underneath the crabs and separate the shells. Remove the feathery gills and intestines. Twist off the claws. Using a cleaver or large knife, cut the crabs in half. Crack the claws using crab crackers or the back of a heavy knife. Soak the noodles in boiling water for 10 minutes, then drain.

Heat a wok, add 2 tablespoons oil, and, when just smoking, add half of the crabs. Stir for 1 minute, reduce the heat to medium, and cover with a lid. Cook for 6 minutes or until the crab shells turn bright red. Lift onto a plate, then repeat with the rest of the crabs, adding 1 tablespoon oil if necessary. Remove the meat from the shells and claws.

Heat the rest of the oil in the wok, then stir-fry the shallots, garlic, and chili for 5 minutes. Add the bean sprouts and pork and cook for 2 minutes. Add the soy sauce, oyster sauce, noodles, crabmeat, and cilantro and stir until heated through. Season with salt, then serve.

Serves 4

Fusilli with tuna, capers, and parsley

15-oz. can tuna in spring water, drained
2 tablespoons olive oil
2 garlic cloves, finely chopped
2 small red chilies, finely chopped
3 tablespoons capers, rinsed and squeezed dry
½ cup chopped parsley
¼ cup lemon juice
13 oz. fusilli or other short pasta
½ cup hot chicken stock

Put the tuna in a bowl and flake it lightly with a fork. Combine the oil, garlic, chili, capers, parsley, and lemon juice in a small bowl. Pour the mixture over the tuna and mix lightly. Season well with salt and freshly ground black pepper.

Meanwhile, cook the pasta in a large saucepan of rapidly boiling water for 10 minutes or until al dente. Drain. Toss the tuna mixture through the pasta, adding enough of the hot chicken stock to make it moist (you may not need it all).

Serves 4

Paella

½ cup white wine
1 small red onion, chopped
12–16 black mussels, cleaned
½ cup olive oil
1 small chicken breast fillet, cut into
  bite-size pieces
1 slice bacon, finely chopped
4 garlic cloves, crushed
1 small red pepper, finely chopped
½ small red onion, extra, finely
  chopped
1 ripe tomato, peeled and chopped
3¼ oz. chorizo, thinly sliced
pinch of cayenne pepper
1 cup paella or short-grain rice
¼ teaspoon saffron threads
2 cups chicken stock, heated
½ cup fresh or frozen peas
12 shrimp, peeled and deveined
3½ oz. calamari, cleaned and cut
  into rings
3½ oz. skinless cod fillets, cut into
  bite-size pieces
2 tablespoons chopped parsley

Fish substitution
  ling, mahimahi, monkfish

Heat the wine and onion in a large saucepan. Add the mussels, cover with a lid, and gently shake the pan for 4–5 minutes over high heat. After 3 minutes, remove any opened mussels from the pan and set them aside. At the end of 5 minutes, discard any unopened mussels. Reserve the cooking liquid.

Heat half the oil in a large frying pan. Pat the chicken dry with paper towels, then cook the chicken for 5 minutes or until golden brown. Remove from the pan and set aside. Heat the remaining oil in the pan, add the bacon, garlic, red pepper, and extra red onion and cook for 5 minutes or until the onion is softened but not browned. Add the tomato, chorizo, and cayenne pepper. Season with salt and freshly ground black pepper. Stir in the reserved cooking liquid, then add the rice and mix well.

Soak the saffron threads in ½ cup of the hot stock, then add it, along with the remaining stock, to the rice and mix well. Bring slowly to a boil. Reduce the heat to low and simmer, uncovered, for 15 minutes, without stirring.

Put the peas, chicken, shrimp, calamari, and fish on top of the rice. Using a wooden spoon, push pieces of the seafood into the rice, cover, and cook over low heat for 10 minutes or until the rice is tender and the seafood is cooked. Add the mussels for the last 5 minutes to heat through. If the rice is not quite cooked, add a little extra stock and cook for a few more minutes. Leave to cool for 5 minutes, then sprinkle with parsley and serve.

Serves 4–6

Kedgeree

12 oz. undyed smoked haddock
3 slices of lemon
1 bay leaf
1 1/4 cups milk
3/4 cup long-grain rice
4 tablespoons butter
1 small onion, finely chopped
2 teaspoons mild curry powder
1 tablespoon finely chopped parsley
3 eggs, hard-boiled, roughly chopped
2/3 cup heavy cream
mango chutney, to serve

Fish substitution
  smoked cod fillets

Put the smoked haddock in a deep frying pan with the lemon and bay leaf, cover with the milk, and simmer for 6 minutes or until cooked through. Remove the fish with a slotted spoon and break into large flakes. Discard any bones.

Put the rice in a saucepan along with 1 1/2 cups water, bring to a boil, cover, and cook for 10 minutes or until just cooked—there should be steam holes in the rice. Drain any excess water and fluff up the rice with a fork.

Melt the butter in a frying pan over medium heat. Add the onion and cook for 3 minutes or until soft. Add the curry powder and cook for another 2 minutes. Add the rice and carefully stir through, cooking for 2–3 minutes or until heated through. Add the fish, parsley, egg, and cream and stir until heated through. Season well with pepper. Serve immediately with mango chutney.

Serves 4

Spaghetti marinara

Tomato sauce
2 tablespoons olive oil
1 onion, finely chopped
1 carrot, finely chopped
2 garlic cloves, crushed
14-oz. can chopped tomatoes
½ cup white wine
1 teaspoon sugar

¼ cup white wine
¼ cup fish stock
1 garlic clove, crushed
12 black mussels, cleaned
13 oz. spaghetti
2 tablespoons butter
4½ oz. calamari, cleaned and cut
  into rings
4½ oz. skinless cod fillet, cut into
  bite-size pieces
7 oz. shrimp, peeled and deveined
⅓ cup Italian parsley, chopped
7-oz. can clams, drained

Fish substitution

  haddock, monkfish, plaice, or any
  firm white fish

To make the tomato sauce, heat the oil in a saucepan, then cook the onion and carrot over medium heat for 10 minutes or until lightly browned. Add the garlic, tomatoes, wine, and sugar, bring to a boil, then reduce the heat and gently simmer for 30 minutes, stirring occasionally.

Heat the wine, stock, and garlic in a large saucepan. Add the mussels. Cover and shake the pan over high heat for 5 minutes. After 3 minutes, remove any opened mussels and set them aside. After 5 minutes, discard any unopened mussels and reserve the cooking liquid.

Cook the spaghetti in a large pot of boiling water until al dente. Drain and keep warm.

Meanwhile, melt the butter in a frying pan over medium heat and stir-fry the calamari, cod, and shrimp in batches for 2 minutes or until just cooked. Remove from the heat and add to the tomato sauce along with the reserved cooking liquid, mussels, parsley, and clams. Gently heat through, then toss the sauce with the pasta and serve.

Serves 4

Fried rice

2 eggs, lightly beaten
2 tablespoons vegetable oil
1 onion, cut into wedges
9 oz. sliced ham, cut into thin strips
4 cups cold, cooked long-grain rice
(see Note)
¼ cup frozen peas
2 tablespoons soy sauce
4 scallions, cut diagonally into short
lengths
9 oz. cooked small shrimp, peeled
and deveined

Season the eggs with salt and freshly ground black pepper.

Heat 1 tablespoon of the oil in a wok or large frying pan and add the eggs, pulling the set egg toward the center and tilting the pan to let the unset egg run to the edges. When almost set, break up into large pieces, to resemble scrambled eggs. Transfer to a plate and set aside.

Heat the remaining oil in the wok, swirling to coat the base and side. Add the onion and stir-fry over high heat until it starts to turn opaque. Add the ham and stir for 1 minute. Stir in the rice and peas and keep stirring for about 3 minutes or until heated through. Add the egg, soy sauce, scallions, and shrimp and stir until heated through, then serve.

Serves 4

Note: Cook the rice a day in advance. Drain, cover, and chill.

Mexican-style paella

1 large garlic clove, peeled
1 small onion, quartered
2 firm tomatoes
1 small red pepper, quartered
¼ cup olive oil
1½ slices bacon, chopped
1⅓ cups long-grain white rice
2½ cups hot fish stock or water
2 poblano chilies, canned or fresh, finely shredded
16 tiger shrimp, peeled and deveined, tails intact
9 oz. skinless snapper fillet, cut into bite-size chunks
2 tablespoons chopped cilantro leaves
1 lime, cut into 4 wedges

Fish substitution
snook, gurnard, cod, halibut, or other firm white fish; jumbo shrimp

Dry-fry the garlic, onion, tomatoes, and pepper in a large, heavy-based frying pan for 45 minutes over low heat until browned all over, turning occasionally. Cool slightly. When cool enough to handle, peel the tomatoes and pepper and roughly chop the flesh. Put in a food processor with the garlic and onion and blend to a puree.

Heat the oil in a deep sauté or frying pan. Add the bacon and cook until crisp. Add the rice and cook for a minute, stirring the grains to make sure they are all coated in oil.

Add the pureed vegetable mixture and cook for 3 minutes. Pour in the stock and 1 teaspoon salt. Bring to a boil and stir once. Reduce the heat to low and cover with a lid. Cook gently for 15 minutes. Add the chili, shrimp, and fish to the pan and cook for another 5 minutes. Add a little hot water to the rice if it becomes too dry. Season with salt if necessary. Sprinkle with cilantro and serve with lime wedges.

Serves 4

Smoked salmon pasta

1 tablespoon olive oil
1 garlic clove, crushed
1½ cups cream
3 tablespoons chopped chives,
  plus extra for serving
¼ teaspoon mustard powder
7 oz. smoked salmon, cut into strips
2 teaspoons lemon juice
1 lb. 2 oz. fettucine or other long,
  flat pasta
3 tablespoons sun-dried tomatoes,
  chopped
2 tablespoons grated Parmesan
  cheese, for serving

Fish substitution
  smoked trout

Heat the oil in a frying pan, then add the garlic. Cook it briefly over low heat, making sure it doesn't burn. Add the cream, chives, and mustard powder. Season to taste with salt and freshly ground black pepper, then bring to a boil. Reduce the heat and simmer, stirring often, until the sauce thickens. Add the strips of salmon and lemon juice and stir until heated through.

Meanwhile, add the fettucine to a large pan of boiling water and cook until al dente. Drain well and return to the same pan. Toss the sauce through the pasta, then divide among four bowls. Top with the tomatoes, Parmesan, and extra chives.

Serves 4

Saffron shrimp risotto

¼ teaspoon saffron threads
¼ cup olive oil
2 garlic cloves, crushed
3 tablespoons chopped parsley
1 lb. 2 oz. shrimp, peeled and
  deveined, tails intact
¼ cup dry sherry
¼ cup white wine
6 cups fish stock
1 onion, chopped
2 cups risotto rice

Soak the saffron threads in ¼ cup hot water.

Heat half the oil in a large saucepan. Add the garlic, parsley, and shrimp and season with salt and pepper. Cook for 2 minutes, then add the sherry, wine, and saffron with the liquid. Remove the shrimp with a slotted spoon and set aside. Simmer until the liquid has reduced by half. Pour in the stock and 1 cup water, cover, and keep at a constant simmer.

In another large, heavy-based saucepan, heat the remaining oil. Cook the onion for 3 minutes or until golden. Add the rice and stir over medium heat for 3 minutes.

Add ½ cup stock to the rice and stir constantly over low heat until all the liquid has been absorbed. Add ½ cup stock and repeat the process until all the stock has been added and the rice is tender and creamy— this will take 25–30 minutes. Add the shrimp and stir until heated through. Season, then serve.

Serves 4

Asian shrimp and noodle salad

Dressing
2 tablespoons grated fresh ginger
2 tablespoons soy sauce
2 tablespoons sesame oil
1/3 cup red wine vinegar
1 tablespoon sweet chili sauce
2 garlic cloves, crushed
1/3 cup kecap manis

9 oz. dried instant egg noodles
1 lb. 2 oz. cooked jumbo shrimp,
  peeled and deveined, tails intact
5 scallions, sliced diagonally
2 tablespoons chopped cilantro
  leaves
1 red pepper, diced
1/2 cup snow peas, cut into halves
lime wedges, for serving

For the dressing, whisk together the ginger, soy sauce, sesame oil, red wine vinegar, chili sauce, garlic, and kecap manis in a large bowl.

Cook the egg noodles in a large saucepan of boiling water for 2 minutes or until tender, then drain thoroughly. Cool in a large bowl.

Add the dressing, shrimp, and remaining ingredients to the noodles and toss gently. Serve with lime wedges.

Serves 4

Phad Thai

10 tiger shrimp or 20 small shrimp,
  peeled and deveined
7 oz. dried rice noodles
1 tablespoon dried shrimp
¼ cup vegetable oil
2 large eggs, lightly beaten
2 garlic cloves, crushed
1 small red chili, finely chopped
2 tablespoons brown sugar
¼ cup lime juice
2 tablespoons fish sauce
⅓ cup roughly chopped roasted
  peanuts
3 scallions, sliced diagonally
2½ oz. bean sprouts, trimmed
3 tablespoons cilantro leaves
lemon or lime wedges, for serving

Fish substitution
  any other raw shrimp, small scallops

If using tiger shrimp, chop each one into three or four pieces, depending on their size.

Soak the rice noodles and dried shrimp in separate bowls of boiling water for 10 minutes. Drain.

Heat the oil in a wok until smoking. Add the beaten eggs and leave to cook for 30 seconds, then stir to break into small pieces. Add the garlic, chili, and chopped tiger shrimp and cook for 15 seconds, stirring all the time.

Add the sugar, lime juice, and fish sauce and cook for 15 seconds, stirring and tossing in the wok. Add the noodles, 3 tablespoons of the peanuts, and the shrimp. Toss together in the wok to heat through, then add the scallions and bean sprouts. Cook for another 30 seconds, then put on a serving plate and sprinkle with the remaining peanuts and the cilantro leaves. Serve immediately with the lemon or lime wedges.

Serves 2

Risotto nero

4 cups fish stock
7 tablespoons butter
1 red onion, finely chopped
2 calamari, cleaned, heads discarded,
   tentacles set aside, and bodies
   finely chopped
2 garlic cloves, crushed
1½ cups risotto rice
3 sachets of squid or cuttlefish ink,
   or the ink sacs from the squid
½ cup plus 2 tablespoons white wine
2 teaspoons olive oil

Pour the stock into a saucepan, bring to a boil, then keep at a low simmer.

Heat the butter in a large, wide, heavy-based saucepan and cook the onion until softened but not browned. Increase the heat and add the calamari. Cook for 4 minutes or until the calamari turns opaque. Add the garlic and stir briefly. Add the rice and reduce the heat to low. Season and stir briefly to thoroughly coat the rice.

Squeeze out the ink from the sachets and add to the rice with the wine. Increase the heat and stir until all the liquid has been absorbed.

Stir in a ladleful of the simmering stock and cook over medium heat, stirring continuously. When the stock has been absorbed, stir in another ladleful. Continue like this for about 20 minutes or until the rice is al dente. You may not need to use all the stock, or you may need a little extra—every risotto will be slightly different.

Heat the olive oil in a frying pan and fry the tentacles quickly; they should turn opaque and brown a little. Garnish the risotto with the tentacles and serve immediately.

Serves 6 as an appetizer

Clams with spaghettini

3 lb. 5 oz. live clams in the shell,
  cleaned
2 tablespoons olive oil
1 onion, finely chopped
2 large garlic cloves, crushed
1½ cups button mushrooms, thinly
  sliced
½ cup dry white wine
3 medium ripe tomatoes, peeled
  and chopped
1 tablespoon tomato paste
pinch of sugar
1 lb. 2 oz. spaghettini or other long,
  thin pasta
2 tablespoons chopped parsley

Fish substitution
  cockles

Put the clams in a large saucepan,
heat over medium heat, and cover
with a lid. Cook for 5 minutes. Discard
any that have not opened. Strain the
liquid into a bowl. Remove the clams
from their shells and set aside.

Meanwhile, heat the oil in a wide,
shallow saucepan or deep frying pan
and add the onion and garlic. Cook
over medium heat for 5 minutes or
until the onion is soft, then add the
mushrooms and cook for another
5 minutes, stirring now and then,
until they are cooked through. Pour
the wine into the pan and allow to
bubble for a couple of minutes. Add
the tomatoes and their juices, the
tomato paste, sugar, and the cooking
juices from the clams. Bring to a boil,
reduce the heat to medium, and
cook at a steady simmer, without a
lid, for 20 minutes to allow the excess
liquid to evaporate and the sauce to
thicken. Heat a large pot of water to
a boil for the pasta.

Add the clams to the sauce and
gently heat through. Cook the pasta
for 4–5 minutes or until al dente,
drain, and return to the pan. Stir the
parsley into the sauce, season, and
pour over the pasta. Toss together
and serve in large, warm bowls.

Serves 4

Shrimp jambalaya

2 lb. 4 oz. jumbo shrimp, peeled and
  deveined, heads, shells, and tails
  reserved
2 small onions, chopped
2 celery stalks, chopped
1 cup dry white wine
¼ cup vegetable oil
7 oz. chorizo or spicy sausage,
  chopped
1 red pepper, chopped
14-oz. can chopped tomatoes
½ teaspoon cayenne pepper
¼ teaspoon dried thyme
¼ teaspoon dried oregano
2 cups long-grain rice

Put the shrimp heads, shells, and tails
in a saucepan with half of the onion,
half the celery, the wine, and 4 cups
water. Bring to a boil, then reduce
the heat and simmer for 20 minutes.
Strain through a fine sieve, reserving
the shrimp stock.

Heat the oil in a large, heavy-based
frying pan and cook the sausage for
5 minutes or until browned. Remove
from the pan with a slotted spoon and
set aside.

Add the remaining onion and celery
and the chopped red pepper to the
pan and cook, stirring occasionally,
for 5 minutes. Add the tomatoes,
cayenne pepper, dried herbs, and
½ teaspoon freshly ground black
pepper and bring to a boil. Reduce
the heat and simmer, covered, for
10 minutes. Return the sausage to
the pan and add the rice and shrimp
stock. Bring back to a boil, reduce
the heat, and simmer, covered, for
25 minutes or until almost all the
liquid has been absorbed and the
rice is tender. Add the shrimp and stir
through gently. Cover and cook for
another 5 minutes or until the shrimp
are pink and cooked through.

Serves 6

Fancy fish

Chermoula snapper

Chermoula
½ cup olive oil
2 garlic cloves, crushed
¼ teaspoon cayenne pepper
1 teaspoon paprika
2 teaspoons ground cumin
2 tablespoons lemon juice
5 tablespoons finely chopped cilantro
   leaves

2 lb. 4 oz. skinless snapper fillets
lemon wedges, for serving

Fish substitution
   bass, gray mullet, grouper, red
   emperor

To make the chermoula, mix the olive oil with the garlic, cayenne pepper, paprika, cumin, lemon juice, cilantro, and ¼ teaspoon salt. Place the fish fillets skin-side down in a large dish or on a tray. Brush the chermoula over the fish fillets, using up all the mixture, and leave them to marinate in the fridge for 1–2 hours, or overnight if time permits.

Preheat a broiler. Shake any loose bits of marinade off the fish and put the fillets on a foil-lined baking tray. Cook for 7–10 minutes or until lightly golden on top and cooked through. Season and serve with lemon wedges.

Serves 4

Mahimahi with lime sauce

4 (7-oz.) skinless mahimahi fillets
zest and juice of 2 limes
½ cup dry white wine
1 large garlic clove, cut into slivers
1 cup unsalted butter, chilled
2 tablespoons vegetable oil

Fish substitution
   sea bass, pompano, snapper,
   cod, John Dory

Put the fish fillets in a nonmetallic dish. Mix the lime zest and juice, wine, and garlic together and pour over the fish. Turn the fish and leave to marinate for 30 minutes, turning now and then. Meanwhile, cut the butter into cubes and return to the fridge.

Transfer the fish to a plate. Strain the marinade through a sieve into a small saucepan. Bring the marinade to a boil and simmer until reduced to 2 tablespoons.

Meanwhile, heat the oil in a large frying pan. When hot, add half of the fish and cook for 3–4 minutes, turning once, or until opaque and cooked through. Repeat with the rest of the fish and keep warm in the oven.

Over low heat, whisk the butter, cube by cube, into the liquid left in the saucepan, whisking thoroughly after each addition. When half of the butter has been incorporated, a few cubes can be added at a time. Do not allow the sauce to overheat. When all the butter has been incorporated, season to taste. Serve the sauce with the fish.

Serves 4

Fruits de mer with herb aioli

Herb aioli
4 egg yolks
4 garlic cloves, crushed
1 tablespoon chopped basil
4 tablespoons chopped Italian parsley
1 tablespoon lemon juice
scant 1 cup olive oil

1 cup dry white wine
1 cup fish stock
pinch of saffron threads
1 bay leaf
4 black peppercorns
2 raw lobster tails, meat removed,
   shells reserved
12 black mussels, cleaned
9 oz. scallops, in their shells, cleaned
1 lb. 2 oz. shrimp, peeled and
   deveined, tails intact
4 (1^3/$_4$-oz.) skinless salmon fillets
lemon wedges, for serving

To make the herb aioli, put the egg yolks, garlic, basil, parsley, and lemon juice in a mortar and pestle or food processor and pound or mix until light and creamy. Add the oil, drop by drop, from the tip of a spoon, pounding or processing constantly until the mixture begins to thicken, then add the oil in a very thin stream. (If you are using a food processor, pour in the oil in a thin stream with the motor running.)

Pour the wine and stock into a frying pan and add the saffron, bay leaf, and peppercorns. Bring the liquid to a very slow simmer. Add the lobster meat and poach for 5 minutes or until opaque, then remove from the pan with tongs or a slotted spoon, cover, and keep warm. Poach the remaining seafood separately in batches. The mussels and scallops will take about 2 minutes to cook and open (discard any mussels that have not opened in this time). The shrimp will take 3 minutes and should turn pink, and the salmon will take a little longer, depending on the thickness of the fillets.

Cut the lobster into thick medallions, trim and rinse the lobster shells, and arrange the meat back in the shells. Put the scallops back in their shells. Arrange the seafood on a large platter, keeping each type together. If you like, you can line the platter with rock salt to hold the shells steady. Scoop the aioli into a small bowl and put it in the center of the platter. Serve with lemon wedges and provide plenty of napkins, as this can get a bit messy.

Serves 4

Classic Venetian-style marinated sole

1 lb. 2 oz. skinless sole fillets
heaping 1/3 cup all-purpose flour
5–6 tablespoons olive oil
1 tablespoon raisins or sultanas
1 large onion, thinly sliced
1/2 cup plus 2 tablespoons red
  wine vinegar
1/2 cup dry white wine
1 cinnamon stick
2 tablespoons pine nuts
pared zest of a small orange, in strips
4 bay leaves

Fish substitution

  flounder, lemon sole, Dover sole,
  John Dory, turbot

Lightly dust the fish fillets with the flour. Heat 3 tablespoons of the oil in a large frying pan and cook the fish in batches until lightly golden and crisp. Add another tablespoon of oil if necessary. Drain on crumpled paper towels. Arrange the fish in a single layer in a serving dish. Wipe out the frying pan.

Put the raisins in a cup, cover with warm water, and leave to soak. Heat the remaining olive oil in the frying pan and add the onion. Reduce the temperature to low and cover with a lid. Gently stew the onion for 20–25 minutes or until soft and translucent, stirring occasionally. Increase the heat and add the vinegar, wine, and cinnamon stick. Boil for 3 minutes. Take the pan off the heat, drain the raisins, and add to the pan along with the pine nuts, orange zest, and a little salt and freshly ground black pepper.

Pour the marinade over the fish and tuck the bay leaves among the fillets. Cool, then cover and refrigerate for twenty-four hours. Serve at room temperature.

Serves 4

Sole Normande

2 cups dry white wine
12 oysters, shucked
12 shrimp, peeled and deveined
12 small button mushrooms or
    6 medium mushrooms, halved
4 skinless sole fillets
1 cup cream
1 truffle, thinly sliced
1 tablespoon chopped parsley

Pour the wine into a deep frying pan and bring to a boil. Add the oysters to the wine and poach for 2–3 minutes, then lift out with a slotted spoon, drain, and keep warm. Poach the shrimp in the wine for 3 minutes or until pink and cooked through. Lift out and keep warm. Poach the mushrooms for 5 minutes, then lift out and keep warm. Add the sole fillets to the poaching liquid and cook for 5 minutes or until the flesh is cooked through and opaque. Lift out onto a serving dish, cover, and keep warm.

Pour the cream into the poaching liquid and bring to a boil. Boil until the sauce has reduced by half and thickened enough to coat the back of a spoon. Season with salt and freshly ground black pepper.

Put a sole fillet on each plate and sprinkle with the shrimp, oysters, and mushrooms, then pour the sauce over the top. Sprinkle with the sliced truffle and parsley and serve immediately.

Serves 4

Grilled slipper lobsters with foaming citrus butter

2 lb. 4 oz. slipper lobsters
4 tablespoons butter
1 large garlic clove, crushed
1 tablespoon finely grated orange zest
1 tablespoon orange juice
1 tablespoon lemon juice
1 tablespoon finely chopped chives
sourdough bread, for serving

Fish substitution
lobster tails, crayfish

Freeze the lobsters for an hour to immobilize them, then plunge into boiling water for 2 minutes. Drain. Using a sharp knife or cleaver, cut each lobster in half. Put them on a large baking tray, cut-side up, and cook under a hot broiler for 3 minutes, then turn and cook for another 3 minutes or until the flesh is white and opaque.

Melt the butter in a small saucepan and, when sizzling, add the garlic. Cook for 1 minute, stirring. Add the zest and juices to the garlic butter and bring to a boil again. Add the chives and season with salt and freshly ground black pepper.

Serve each person some lobster halves and a small bowl of the hot, foaming butter for dipping. Serve with sourdough bread to mop up the citrus butter.

Serves 4

Teppan yaki with dipping sauces

Scallion dipping sauce
1 scallion, finely chopped
1/4 cup soy sauce
1 tablespoon mirin
1 tablespoon sugar

Sesame dipping sauce
2 tablespoons crushed white
  sesame seeds
2 teaspoons sugar
1/4 cup soy sauce
1 tablespoon mirin
1 teaspoon bonito-flavored soup
  stock

vegetable oil, for greasing
4 scallions, cut into 2½-inch lengths
1 small red pepper, cut into thin
  strips
1 small orange pepper, cut into
  thin strips
8 small shiitake mushrooms, stalks
  trimmed and caps halved
14-oz. salmon fillet, cut into bite-size
  cubes
16 shrimp, peeled and deveined,
  tails intact
14 oz. cleaned baby calamari
lemon wedges, for serving

Fish substitution
  lobster, abalone, oysters

Prepare the dipping sauces first. For the scallion sauce, mix the scallion, soy sauce, mirin, and sugar together, then pour into a dipping bowl. For the sesame sauce, mix the crushed sesame seeds, sugar, soy sauce, mirin, stock, and 1 tablespoon hot water together, then pour into a dipping bowl. Set both the bowls aside until needed.

Preheat a large frying pan until hot and grease with a little oil. Add half of the scallions, pepper strips, and mushrooms to the pan and cook for a few minutes, turning to ensure even cooking. When the vegetables are nearly cooked, push them to the edges of the pan or remove to a plate and keep warm in the oven while you cook all the seafood.

Add half of the salmon cubes to the pan and cook for 1 minute, then add half of the shrimp. Cook for 1 minute, then add half of the calamari. Continue cooking for 2 minutes or until the seafood is cooked, making sure you turn the seafood to cook all over. Add a little more oil if needed.

Serve the seafood and vegetables together with the dipping sauces, the lemon wedges, and some rice. Repeat the cooking order with the rest of the ingredients.

Serves 4

Note: Teppan yaki is usually eaten at specialty restaurants. The chefs work at grills around which the diners sit. The food is cooked in batches and served as it is cooked. When serving this dish at home, you can cook it all at once or serve it in batches.

Greek-style calamari

Stuffing
1 tablespoon olive oil
2 scallions, chopped
1 1/2 cups cold, cooked rice (see Note)
1/2 cup pine nuts
1/2 cup currants
2 tablespoons chopped parsley
2 teaspoons finely grated lemon zest
1 egg, lightly beaten

2 lb. 4 oz. calamari tubes, washed
  and patted dry

Sauce
4 large, ripe tomatoes
1 tablespoon olive oil
1 onion, finely chopped
1 garlic clove, crushed
1/4 cup good-quality red wine
1 tablespoon chopped fresh oregano

Preheat the oven to 315°F. For the stuffing, mix the oil, scallions, rice, pine nuts, currants, parsley, and lemon zest in a bowl. Season well with salt and freshly ground black pepper. Add enough egg to moisten all the ingredients. Fill each calamari tube three-quarters full with the stuffing. Secure the ends with toothpicks. Put in a single layer in a casserole dish.

For the sauce, score a cross in the base of each tomato, put in a bowl of boiling water for 30 seconds, then plunge into cold water and peel the skin away from the cross. Chop the flesh. Heat the oil in a pan, then add the onion and garlic and cook over low heat for 2 minutes or until the onion is soft. Add the tomatoes, wine, and oregano and bring to a boil. Reduce the heat, cover, and cook over low heat for 10 minutes.

Pour the hot sauce over the calamari, cover, and bake for 20 minutes or until the calamari is tender. Remove the toothpicks before cutting into thick slices for serving. Spoon the sauce over the calamari just before serving.

Serves 4–6

Note: You will need to cook 1/2 cup rice for this recipe.

Salmon in nori with noodles

4 salmon cutlets, cut from the
  center of the fish
1 sheet of nori (dried seaweed)
2 teaspoons vegetable oil
9 oz. somen noodles
2 scallions, cut into long, thin strips

Dressing
1/2–3/4 teaspoon wasabi paste,
  to taste
2 tablespoons rice vinegar
2 tablespoons mirin
1 tablespoon lime juice
2 teaspoons brown sugar
1 tablespoon vegetable oil
2 teaspoons soy sauce
2 teaspoons black sesame seeds,
  plus some extra for garnish

Fish substitution
  ocean trout

Remove the skin and bones from the salmon, keeping the cutlets in one piece. Cut the nori into strips and wrap a strip tightly around each cutlet to form a neat circle. Seal the edges with a little water. Season with salt and freshly ground black pepper.

Heat the oil in a frying pan and cook the salmon for 2–3 minutes on each side or until cooked to your liking (ideally, it should be a little pink in the center).

While the salmon is cooking, prepare the noodles and dressing. Put the noodles in a large bowl, cover with boiling water, and let stand for 5 minutes or until softened. Drain well. Combine the dressing ingredients in a bowl and mix well.

Divide the noodles among four serving plates, top with a salmon cutlet, and drizzle with the dressing. Add the scallions, then sprinkle with the extra sesame seeds.

Serves 4

Note: Several of the ingredients in this recipe are Japanese, so you may need to get them from an Asian market.

Fritto misto di mare

Garlic and anchovy sauce
½ cup extra-virgin olive oil
2 garlic cloves, crushed
3 anchovy fillets, finely chopped
2 tablespoons finely chopped parsley
pinch of chili flakes

Batter
1⅔ cups all-purpose flour
⅓ cup olive oil
1 large egg white

9 oz. baby calamari, cleaned
12 large shrimp, peeled and
   deveined, tails intact
8 small octopuses, cleaned
16 scallops, cleaned
12 fresh sardines, gutted and heads
   removed
9 oz. skinless ling fillets, cut into
   large cubes
vegetable oil, for deep-frying
lemon wedges, for serving

Fish substitution
   cod, snapper

To make the sauce, warm the oil in a frying pan. Add the garlic, anchovies, parsley, and chili flakes. Cook over low heat for 1 minute or until the garlic is soft but not brown. Serve warm or chilled.

To make the batter, sift the flour into a bowl and stir in ¼ teaspoon salt. Mix in the oil with a wooden spoon, then gradually add 1¼ cups lukewarm water, whisking when the mixture becomes liquid. Continue whisking until the batter is smooth and thick. Cover and leave to stand for 20 minutes in the fridge. Whisk the egg white until stiff peaks form, then fold gently into the batter. Fill a deep frying pan one-third full of oil and heat to 375°F or until a piece of white bread fries golden in 10 seconds.

Dry the seafood on paper towels. Working with one type of seafood at a time, dip it in the batter. Shake off the excess batter, then lower into the oil, in batches if necessary. Be careful of the seafood splattering when it hits the oil. Deep-fry for 2–3 minutes or until golden and crisp. Drain on crumpled paper towels, then keep warm in a 200°F oven (but don't crowd the seafood or it will get soggy). Sprinkle with salt and serve with the lemon wedges and the sauce.

Serves 4

Banana leaf steamed fish with fresh sambal

1 lb. 12 oz. whole snapper, scaled, fins removed, and gutted
2 lengths of banana leaf, each measuring approximately 24 x 16 inches (see Notes)
2 tablespoons unsalted peanuts
3 red Asian shallots, peeled
1 stem of lemongrass (white part only), cut into 3 pieces
small knob of fresh galangal, peeled
1 teaspoon brown sugar
¼ cup vegetable oil
½ teaspoon ground turmeric
1 tablespoon tamarind puree
1 tablespoon fish sauce
1 teaspoon sambal oelek or other chili paste
¼ cup coconut milk
4 kaffir lime leaves (see Notes)

Sambal
1 small mango, peeled, stone removed, and cut into small dice
1 small red chili, deseeded and finely chopped
2 tablespoons shredded fresh or dried coconut
1 tablespoon lime juice

Fish substitution
sea bass, coral trout

Score the fish with diagonal cuts on both sides.

If the banana leaf has been frozen, it will be soft when defrosted, but if fresh and tough, blanch in boiling water for a minute to soften, then drain and rinse in cold water. Pat dry and place one of the pieces of leaf on top of the other so that they overlap by 4 inches. Place the fish on top of the leaves. Alternatively, put the fish on a piece of foil.

Toast the peanuts in a warm oven or in a saucepan over a low heat until golden. Allow to cool. Put the shallots, lemongrass, galangal, and sugar in a food processor and whizz together to chop finely. Otherwise, chop and mix by hand. Heat the oil in a saucepan and, when hot, add the chopped shallot mixture. Cook for 5 minutes, stirring, then add the turmeric, tamarind, fish sauce, sambal oelek, and coconut milk and remove from the heat. Allow to cool for 5 minutes, then spoon half of the mixture inside the cavity of the fish and the rest on the top.

Roughly chop the toasted peanuts, then sprinkle them over the fish with the lime leaves. Wrap the fish in the leaf or foil to make a parcel. Steam or barbecue for 25 minutes.

Meanwhile, make the sambal by mixing all the ingredients together, then serve with the cooked fish.

Serves 2

Notes: If you don't have access to a banana tree, frozen banana leaves can often be found in the freezer section of Asian markets. Failing that, heavy-duty foil can be used instead.

Kaffir lime leaves are quite unusual in that they have double leaves joined together at the tip—they resemble an elongated figure eight. Usually, the leaves have broken into halves by the time they reach the supermarket.

Turbot en papillote with sorrel

2 tablespoons butter
1 small onion, finely chopped
1/2 cup dry white wine
2/3 cup fish stock
2 teaspoons vegetable oil, for
  greasing
3 lb. 5 oz. whole turbot, filleted
  into 4 pieces
2 1/2 tablespoons crème fraîche
3 tablespoons chopped sorrel or
  basil leaves

Fish substitution

pompano, flounder, lemon sole,
Dover sole

Melt the butter in a saucepan and add the onion. Cook for 10 minutes or until softened but not browned, stirring now and then. Pour in the wine and stock and bring to a boil. Allow to boil for 10–15 minutes or until reduced by half—you should end up with about 1/2 cup.

Preheat the oven to 350°F. Cut four 12-inch-diameter circles from baking parchment. Lightly oil the circles, fold in half to make a crease along the middle, and then unfold. Place a piece of fish on one half of each circle.

Once the sauce has reduced, add the crème fraîche. Stir, allow to bubble for 30 seconds, then remove from the heat. Season, stir in the sorrel, and then spoon a quarter of the sauce over the first piece of fish. Fold the empty half of the circle over the fish, fold the edges of the circle over twice, and pinch together to seal. Repeat with the other pieces of turbot. As you make the parcels, place them on a large baking tray. Bake the fish for 15–20 minutes, depending on the thickness of the fish. Put the parcels on plates so they can be opened at the table.

Serves 4

Zarzuela

Sofrito base
1 tablespoon olive oil
2 onions, finely chopped
2 large tomatoes, peeled, deseeded,
  and chopped
1 tablespoon tomato paste

Picada sauce
3 slices of white bread, crusts
  removed
1 tablespoon almonds, toasted
3 garlic cloves
1 tablespoon olive oil

1 raw lobster tail (about 14 oz.)
1 lb. 10 oz. skinless monkfish fillets
all-purpose flour, seasoned with salt
  and pepper
2–3 tablespoons olive oil
4½ oz. calamari, cleaned and cut
  into rings
12 large shrimp
½ cup dry white wine
12–15 black mussels, cleaned
½ cup brandy
3 tablespoons chopped parsley

Fish substitution
  cod, warehou, shark, or any firm
  white fish

To make the sofrito base, heat the oil in a large, flameproof casserole dish on the stovetop. Add the onion and stir for 5 minutes without browning. Add the tomatoes, tomato paste, and ½ cup water and cook, stirring, for 10 minutes. Stir in another ½ cup water, season, and set the dish aside.

For the picada sauce, finely chop the bread, almonds, and garlic in a food processor or by hand. With the motor running, or stirring continuously, gradually add the oil to form a paste.

Preheat the oven to 350°F. Cut the lobster tail into rounds through the membrane that separates the shell segments, then set aside. Cut the fish fillets into bite-size pieces and lightly coat in flour. Heat the oil in a large frying pan and fry the fish in batches over medium heat for 2–3 minutes or until cooked and golden brown all over. Transfer to the casserole dish with the sofrito.

Add a little oil to the pan if necessary, add the calamari, and cook, stirring, for 1–2 minutes. Remove and add to the casserole. Cook the lobster and shrimp for 2–3 minutes or until just pink, then add to the casserole. Add the wine to the pan and bring to a boil. Reduce the heat, add the mussels, cover, and steam for

4–5 minutes. Add to the casserole, discarding any unopened mussels.

Pour the brandy into the pan, ignite carefully with a match, and when the flames have died down, pour over the seafood. Mix well, cover, and bake for 20 minutes. Stir in the picada sauce and cook for another 10 minutes or until warmed through. Do not overcook or the seafood will toughen. Sprinkle with the parsley.

Serves 4–6

Crabs with spices, cilantro, and chilies

4 small live crabs, 9 oz. each, or
   2 crabs, 1 lb. 2 oz. each
1/2 cup vegetable oil
2 garlic cloves, very finely chopped
2 teaspoons finely grated fresh ginger
1/4 teaspoon ground cumin
1/4 teaspoon ground coriander
1/4 teaspoon ground turmeric
1/4 teaspoon cayenne pepper
1 tablespoon tamarind puree
1 teaspoon sugar
2 small red chilies, finely chopped
2 tablespoons chopped cilantro
   leaves

Fish substitution
   large shrimp

Freeze the crabs for 1 hour to immobilize them. Plunge them into boiling water for 2 minutes. Using a large, heavy-bladed knife or cleaver, cut the crabs in half (quarters if you are using the large ones) and scrape out the gray gills, then twist off and crack the claws. Turn the body over and pull off the apron pieces. Rinse under cold running water and pat dry.

Mix together half of the oil, the garlic, ginger, cumin, coriander, turmeric, cayenne pepper, tamarind, sugar, chilies, and a generous pinch of salt. Heat the remaining oil in a large, deep frying pan. When the oil is hot, add the spice mixture and stir over the heat for 30 seconds.

Add the crabs and cook, stirring for 2 minutes, making sure the spice mix gets rubbed into the cut edges of the crabs. Add 2 1/2 tablespoons water, cover, and steam the crabs for another 5–6 minutes or until cooked. The crabs will turn pink or red when they are ready and the flesh will turn opaque. Drizzle a little of the liquid from the pan over the crabs, sprinkle with the cilantro leaves, and serve. Serve with crab crackers, picks, bread, and lots of napkins.

Serves 4

Stir-fried calamari flowers with pepper

14 oz. calamari tubes
1/4 cup vegetable oil
2 tablespoons salted, fermented
  black beans, mashed
1 small onion, cut into small cubes
1 small green pepper, cut into small
  cubes
3–4 small slices of peeled, fresh
  ginger
1 scallion, cut into short lengths
1 small red chili, chopped
1 tablespoon Chinese rice wine
1/2 teaspoon roasted sesame oil

Open up the calamari tubes and
scrub off any soft, jellylike substance,
then score the inside of the flesh with
a fine crisscross pattern, making sure
you do not cut all the way through.
Cut the calamari into pieces of about
1 1/4 x 2 inches.

Blanch the calamari in a saucepan of
boiling water for 25–30 seconds—
each piece will curl up and the
crisscross pattern will open out,
hence the name "flower." Remove
and rinse in cold water, then drain
and dry well.

Heat a wok over high heat, add the
oil, and heat until very hot. Stir-fry the
black beans, onion, green pepper,
ginger, scallion, and chili for 1 minute.
Add the calamari and rice wine, blend
well, and stir for 1 minute. Sprinkle
with the sesame oil.

Serves 4 as an appetizer

Scallops in black bean sauce

24 scallops, cleaned
2 tablespoons vegetable oil
1 tablespoon soy sauce
2 tablespoons Chinese rice wine
1 teaspoon sugar
1 garlic clove, finely chopped
1 scallion, finely chopped
1/2 teaspoon finely grated fresh ginger
1 tablespoon salted fermented
   black beans, rinsed and drained
   (see Note)
1 teaspoon roasted sesame oil

Fish substitution

shrimp, crayfish, lobster, baby calamari

Begin by preparing the scallops. Heat 1 tablespoon of the vegetable oil in a wok and, when hot, add the scallops. Cook for 2 minutes or until firm. Remove to a plate.

Mix together the soy sauce, rice wine, and sugar in a cup with a tablespoon of water and set aside.

Add the remaining vegetable oil to the wok and heat until it is beginning to smoke. Add the garlic, scallion, and ginger. Cook for 30 seconds. Add the beans and the soy sauce mixture and bring to a boil. Return the scallops to the sauce with the sesame oil and allow to simmer for about 30 seconds. Serve immediately with rice and steamed vegetables.

Serves 4

Note: Salted fermented black beans are fermented soybeans that have a distinct, salty flavor. They are used in the cooking of southern China.

Red mullet with baked eggplant

4 (7-oz.) red mullets, cleaned

Marinade
pinch of saffron threads
1/2 cup olive oil
2 tablespoons lemon juice
1 tablespoon pomegranate molasses
   (optional, see Note)
1 small onion, grated
1 large garlic clove, crushed
1 tablespoon dried oregano
pinch of crushed dried chili
1 teaspoon nigella seeds or
   1/2 teaspoon cracked black pepper
1 teaspoon coriander seeds, slightly
   crushed
1 teaspoon cumin seeds

12 oz. eggplant, cut into chunks
1/2 cup pine nuts, lightly toasted
3 1/2 oz. baby spinach
2 tablespoons roughly torn mint
1 tablespoon red wine vinegar
16 small, pitted black olives

Fish substitution
   redfish

Lay the fish in a single layer in a shallow, nonmetallic dish. Infuse the saffron in a tablespoon of hot water for 10 minutes. Mix the saffron and its soaking liquid with half of the oil, a generous pinch of salt, and the remaining marinade ingredients. Spread the marinade into the central cavity and over the skin of each fish. Cover and marinate in the fridge for 2 hours.

Transfer the fish to a large baking tray and distribute the eggplant around the fish. Brush the eggplant and fish all over with the remaining marinade. Cook both under a hot broiler, turning now and then, for 20 minutes or until the fish are cooked through.

Meanwhile, put the pine nuts, spinach, and mint in a bowl and toss well. Mix the remaining oil and the vinegar together and season. Dress the salad with the oil and vinegar mixture and divide among four plates. Sprinkle the olives and cooked eggplant over the salad leaves and place the red mullet on top. Drizzle a little of the cooking juices over each fish.

Serves 4

Note: Pomegranate molasses is a syrup with a sweet-and-sour taste.

Lobster Newburg

8 oz. raw lobster meat
4 tablespoons butter, plus extra for
  spreading on the toast
1 tablespoon sherry
1 tablespoon brandy
scant 1 cup heavy cream
4 slices bread
2 large egg yolks
pinch of cayenne pepper, plus a
  little extra for serving

Fish substitution
  shrimp, crab

Cut the lobster into small chunks. Melt the butter in a saucepan and, when hot, add the lobster. Cook for 3–4 minutes or until the lobster is firm and tinged with brown. Mix the sherry and brandy together and pour over the lobster. Carefully light the alcohol with a match and flambé the lobster (keep a saucepan lid nearby in case the flame gets out of hand). Using a slotted spoon, transfer the lobster to a plate and set aside. Add the cream to the pan and stir to heat.

Toast and butter the bread. Remove the crusts and cut each slice in two diagonally so you end up with eight triangles. Keep warm.

Lightly beat the egg yolks with a fork. Add 2 tablespoons of the warm cream mixture to the yolks and mix. Return to the sauce in the pan, whisk well, then put back over low heat and stir for 3–4 minutes to thicken the sauce. The mixture must not overheat or boil or the eggs will scramble. Stir in the lobster and any juices on the plate. Season, add the cayenne pepper, and serve on the triangles of hot, buttered toast or, for a main meal, serve with boiled rice. Sprinkle with a little cayenne pepper before serving.

Serves 4

Crayfish étouffée

2 tomatoes
½ cup vegetable oil
heaping ⅓ cup all-purpose flour
3 cups fish stock
2 large onions, chopped
1 small green pepper, chopped
1 small red pepper, chopped
2½ oz. celery stalks, chopped
1 large garlic clove, finely chopped
½ teaspoon paprika
¼ teaspoon cayenne pepper
1 teaspoon Worcestershire sauce
3 drops hot pepper sauce
2 teaspoons chopped thyme
12 oz. crayfish tails, shells removed
3 scallions, trimmed and chopped
2 tablespoons chopped parsley, plus
   a little extra for garnish

Fish substitution
tiger shrimp, diced raw lobster

Score a cross in the base of each tomato. Cover in boiling water for 30 seconds, then plunge into cold water. Drain and peel the skin away from the cross. Chop the tomatoes, discarding the cores. Set aside until needed.

Begin by making the dark brown roux. Pour the oil into a large, heavy-based saucepan and heat through at a low temperature. Gradually add the flour, bit by bit, stirring between each addition. You will end up with a thin roux. Continue to cook and stir the roux over a low heat until it turns a dark, nutty brown color. This will take 30–40 minutes.

Toward the end of cooking the roux, pour the stock into another saucepan, bring it to a boil, then reduce to a gentle simmer.

Remove the saucepan containing the roux from the heat and immediately stir in the tomatoes, onion, pepper, celery, and garlic—the mixture will sizzle. Continue to stir the mixture for a couple of minutes or until it has cooled down. Add the paprika, cayenne pepper, Worcestershire sauce, hot pepper sauce, thyme, 1½ teaspoons salt, and ¼ teaspoon freshly ground black pepper to the pan and stir to combine.

Return the mixture to a low heat and gradually add the stock, little by little, stirring between each addition. Once all the stock is incorporated, slowly bring to a boil, stirring, then leave on medium–low heat to simmer for 15 minutes. Give it a stir now and then to make sure it does not stick to the bottom of the pan.

Add the crayfish tails and cook gently for 5 minutes or until they have turned opaque and are tinged with pink and orange. Stir in the scallions and parsley and check the seasoning, adding more salt if necessary. Sprinkle with a little extra parsley and serve with rice.

Serves 4

Teriyaki salmon with soba noodles

12 dried shiitake mushrooms
1 teaspoon dashi granules
¼ cup Japanese soy sauce
2 tablespoons mirin
½ teaspoon superfine sugar
4 (5½-oz.) salmon cutlets
¼ cup teriyaki marinade
1 tablespoon honey
1 teaspoon sesame oil
9 oz. dried soba noodles
1 tablespoon vegetable oil
2 scallions, sliced diagonally

Fish substitution
mackerel

Soak the mushrooms in 2 cups boiling water for 10 minutes. Strain, reserving the soaking liquid. Pour the soaking liquid into a saucepan, add the dashi granules, soy sauce, mirin, and sugar, and bring to a boil. Simmer for 5 minutes.

Put the salmon, mushrooms, teriyaki marinade, honey, and sesame oil into a nonmetallic dish and allow to marinate for 15 minutes.

Bring a large saucepan of water to a boil and cook the noodles for 3–4 minutes or until tender. Drain.

Heat the vegetable oil in a preheated grill pan. Take the salmon and mushrooms out of the marinade and cook over high heat for 3 minutes on each side or until the fish is cooked but still slightly rare in the center. Pour the reserved marinade over the fish during cooking.

To serve, divide the noodles among four serving bowls, add the broth from the mushrooms, then top with the salmon and mushrooms and sprinkle with scallions.

Serves 4

355

Chili crab

2 live mud crabs, 2 lb. 4 oz. each
2 tablespoons vegetable oil
1 onion, chopped
4 garlic cloves, crushed
1 tablespoon grated fresh ginger
2 red chilies, finely chopped
14-oz. can chopped tomatoes,
    pureed
1 tablespoon soy sauce
1 tablespoon brown sugar
2 teaspoons clear rice vinegar

Freeze the crabs for about 1 hour to immobilize them. Plunge into boiling water for 2 minutes. Wash well with a stiff brush, then pull the apron off from underneath the crab and separate the shells. Remove the feathery gills and intestines. Twist off the claws. Using a cleaver or a heavy-bladed knife, cut the body into quarters. Crack the claws with a good hit with the back of a cleaver.

Heat a wok until very hot, add the oil, and swirl to coat the inside of the wok. Stir-fry the crab in batches for 2–3 minutes or until bright red. Remove and set aside. Add the onion to the wok and cook for 3 minutes. Add the garlic, ginger, and chilies and cook for 1–2 minutes. Stir in the pureed tomatoes, soy sauce, sugar, vinegar, and $1/2$ cup water. Bring to a boil, then cook for 5 minutes or until the sauce is slightly thickened.

Return the crab to the wok and toss to coat with the sauce. Simmer for 8 minutes or until the crab is cooked, turning often.

Serves 4

Moroccan stuffed sardines

1/3 cup couscous
2 tablespoons olive oil
2 tablespoons chopped dried apricots
1/4 cup raisins
1 tablespoon flaked almonds, toasted
1 tablespoon chopped parsley
1 tablespoon chopped mint
grated zest of 1 orange
2 tablespoons freshly squeezed
　orange juice
1 teaspoon finely chopped preserved
　lemon
1 teaspoon ground cinnamon
1/2 teaspoon harissa
16 whole large sardines, split open
16 large fresh vine leaves or
　preserved vine leaves
1 3/4 cups plain yogurt

Fish substitution
　small herring

Put the couscous in a bowl and add 1 tablespoon of the olive oil and 2 1/2 tablespoons boiling water. Stir and leave for 10 minutes to allow the couscous to absorb the liquid.

Fluff the couscous with a fork and add the apricots, raisins, almonds, parsley, mint, orange zest and juice, preserved lemon, cinnamon, harissa, and the remaining oil. Season with salt and pepper and mix.

Divide the stuffing among the sardines, folding the two sides of each fish together to enclose the couscous mixture inside (save any extra couscous to serve with the sardines). Bring a pan of water to a boil and blanch the vine leaves for 30 seconds—you will need to do this in batches. Pat dry with paper towels. If you are using preserved vine leaves, rinse and dry them. Wrap a vine leaf around each sardine and secure it with a toothpick. Preheat a grill pan or barbecue. Cook the sardines for 6 minutes, turning them over halfway through. Serve each one with a dollop of yogurt and any extra couscous.

Serves 4

Crispy fried fish with chili and cucumber

1 lb. 2 oz. whole pomfret, head intact, scaled and gutted
¼ cup vegetable oil
4 red Asian shallots or 1 small onion, thinly sliced
1 garlic clove, finely chopped
1 teaspoon grated fresh ginger
3 small red chilies, deseeded and finely chopped
2 tablespoons brown sugar
1 tablespoon tamarind puree
zest and juice of 1 lime
2 tablespoons fish sauce
1 large cucumber, peeled and julienned
vegetable oil, for deep-frying
1 tablespoon chopped cilantro leaves

Fish substitution
flounder, snapper, sea bass, bream

Score diagonal cuts on both sides of the fish.

Heat the oil in a wok or sauté pan. When the oil is just beginning to smoke, add the shallots and cook for 2 minutes, stirring, until they begin to soften and color. Add the garlic, ginger, and chilies and cook for another minute or until lightly golden and crisp. Mix the sugar, tamarind, lime juice, and fish sauce together and add to the sauce. Allow to simmer for 30 seconds or until the sauce thickens slightly. Stir in the cucumber and remove from the heat. Transfer the sauce to a small saucepan and set aside. Clean the wok or pan.

Fill the wok or pan 1 inch deep with oil and heat to 350°F or until a cube of white bread dropped in the oil browns in 15 seconds. Lower the fish gently into the oil and cook for 4–5 minutes or until golden and crisp, turning once during cooking. Make sure the skin does not stick to the wok. Spoon the hot oil over the fish as it cooks. Meanwhile, gently reheat the sauce. Drain the fish on paper towels. Drizzle the sauce over the fish, then sprinkle with lime zest and cilantro.

Serves 2

Stir-fried fu-yung lobster

1 lb. lobster meat, cut into pieces
¼ cup Chinese rice wine
1 tablespoon finely chopped fresh
  ginger
12 egg whites
½ teaspoon cream of tartar
3 cups vegetable oil
½ cup chicken stock
¼ teaspoon white pepper
1 teaspoon roasted sesame oil
1 teaspoon cornstarch
3 tablespoons finely chopped
  scallion
2 tablespoons finely chopped
  scallion greens

Put the lobster meat in a bowl with 1 tablespoon of the rice wine, 1 teaspoon ginger, and ½ teaspoon salt and toss lightly to coat. In another bowl, beat the egg whites and cream of tartar until stiff. Fold the lobster into this mixture.

Heat a wok over high heat, add half the vegetable oil and heat until very hot, then add the remaining oil. Pour the lobster mixture into the wok in batches—do not stir the mixture, otherwise it will break up. Gently stir the oil from the bottom of the wok so that the "fu-yung" rise to the surface. Remove each batch as soon as it is set, then drain well. Remove the oil from the wok, saving 2 tablespoons.

Combine the stock, white pepper, sesame oil, cornstarch, the remaining rice wine, and 1 teaspoon of salt.

Reheat the wok over high heat, add the reserved oil, and heat until hot. Stir-fry the scallion and remaining ginger over high heat for 10 seconds. Add the stock mixture and cook, stirring constantly to prevent lumps, until thickened. Add the lobster mixture and carefully toss it in the sauce. Transfer to a platter, sprinkle with the scallion greens, and serve.

Serves 6

Crab bisque

4 tablespoons butter
½ carrot, finely chopped
½ onion, finely chopped
1 celery stalk, finely chopped
1 bay leaf
2 sprigs of thyme
2 lb. 4 oz. live crabs, cleaned and
    claws detached
2 tablespoons tomato paste
2 tablespoons brandy
1 cup plus 2 tablespoons dry
    white wine
4 cups fish stock
¼ cup rice
¼ cup heavy cream
¼ teaspoon cayenne pepper

Heat the butter in a large saucepan. Add the vegetables, bay leaf, and thyme and cook over medium heat for 3 minutes without allowing the vegetables to color. Add the crab claws, legs, and bodies and cook for 5 minutes or until the crab shells turn red. Add the tomato paste, brandy, and white wine and simmer for 2 minutes or until reduced by half.

Add the stock and 2 cups water and bring to a boil. Reduce the heat and simmer for 5 minutes. Remove the shells, leaving the crabmeat in the stock, and reserve the claws to use as a garnish. Finely crush the shells in a mortar and pestle, or in a food processor with a little of the stock.

Return the crushed shells to the soup with the rice. Bring to a boil, reduce the heat, cover, and simmer for about 20 minutes or until the rice is soft.

Immediately strain the bisque into a clean saucepan through a fine sieve lined with damp muslin, pressing down firmly on the solids to extract all the liquid. Add the cream and season with salt and cayenne pepper, then gently reheat. Ladle into warmed soup bowls and garnish with the crab claws.

Serves 4

Salmon on skordalia with saffron-lime butter

Skordalia
1 lb. 2 oz. (about 3 medium)
  potatoes, peeled and diced
3 garlic cloves, finely chopped
juice of 1 lime
1/2 cup milk
1/2 cup plus 2 tablespoons virgin
  olive oil

Saffron-lime butter
7 tablespoons butter
pinch of saffron threads
2 tablespoons lime juice

4 (7-oz.) salmon fillets
2 tablespoons vegetable oil
1 tablespoon lime zest
chervil leaves, for garnish

Fish substitution
  ocean trout

To make the skordalia, bring a large saucepan of water to a boil, add the potatoes, and cook for 10 minutes or until very soft. Drain thoroughly and mash until quite smooth. Stir the garlic, lime juice, and milk into the potatoes, then gradually pour in the olive oil, mixing well with a wooden spoon.

To make the saffron-lime butter, melt the butter in a small saucepan, add the saffron and lime juice, and cook until the butter turns a nutty brown color.

Pat the salmon fillets dry. Heat the vegetable oil in a frying pan and cook the salmon, skin-side down, over high heat for 2–3 minutes on each side or until the skin is crisp and golden. Serve the salmon on a bed of the skordalia with the saffron-lime butter drizzled over the top. Garnish with lime zest and chervil leaves.

Serves 4

Barramundi steaks with shiitake mushrooms

2 tablespoons light soy sauce
2 tablespoons vegetable oil
2 tablespoons Chinese rice wine
  or dry sherry
pinch of sugar
zest and juice of 1 lemon
4 (7-oz.) barramundi steaks
  (see Note)
1 teaspoon roasted sesame oil
1½ cups shiitake mushrooms, sliced
2 scallions, chopped

Fish substitution
  snapper, swordfish, cod, salmon,
  halibut

Mix the soy sauce, oil, rice wine, sugar, and lemon zest and juice together in a measuring cup. Put the fish in a shallow, nonmetallic, ovenproof dish in which they fit snugly in a single layer. Pour the marinade over the fish and turn them once so both sides are coated. Cover and refrigerate for at least 4 hours or overnight, turning occasionally. Return to room temperature. Preheat the oven to 350°F.

Heat the sesame oil in a frying pan and add the mushrooms. Cook, stirring, for 3–4 minutes or until beginning to soften. Add the scallions, stir, and remove from the heat. Sprinkle the mushroom and scallion mixture over the fish and bake, covered with a lid or foil, for 25–30 minutes or until the fish is opaque and firm to the touch. Serve with egg noodles.

Serves 4

Note: Barramundi, a highly valued fish, is found in the rivers, estuaries, and seas of northern Australia. It has firm, white flesh, which goes well with the meaty texture of the shiitake mushrooms.

Sole meunière

4 Dover sole, gutted and dark skin
  removed
¼ cup all-purpose flour
1 cup clarified butter (see Note)
2 tablespoons lemon juice
4 tablespoons chopped parsley
lemon wedges, for serving

Fish substitution
  sole fillets

Pat the fish dry with paper towels, cut the fine bones and frill of skin away from around the edge of the fish, remove the heads if you prefer, and then dust lightly with the flour and season. Heat two thirds of the butter in a frying pan large enough to fit all four fish, or use half the butter and cook the fish in two batches.

Put the fish in the pan, skin-side up, and cook for 4 minutes or until golden, turn over carefully, and cook on the other side for another 4 minutes or until the fish is cooked through (the flesh will feel firm). Lift the fish out onto warm plates, skin-side down, and drizzle with the lemon juice and sprinkle with the parsley. Add the remaining butter to the pan and heat until it browns, but be careful not to overbrown it or the sauce will taste burned. Pour over the fish (it will foam as it mixes with the lemon juice) and serve with lemon wedges and steamed vegetables.

Serves 4

Note: Clarified butter has a higher burning point than other butters. To clarify butter, heat regular butter until liquid. Let sit until the white milk solids settle to the bottom. Use a spoon to skim off any foam, then strain off the golden liquid (the clarified butter), leaving the white solids behind.

Poached Atlantic salmon

5 lb. 8 oz. Atlantic salmon, cleaned
  and scaled
15 cups court bouillon (see Basic
  recipes, p. 392)
½ cucumber, peeled
lemon wedges, for serving
mayonnaise, for serving

Fish substitution
  ocean trout, Pacific salmon,
  sea bass

Put the whole fish in a saucepan, pour in the court bouillon, then cover with a lid. Bring to a boil, reduce the heat, and poach for about 15 minutes or until the dorsal fin can be easily removed and the inside of the salmon looks cooked and opaque. Alternatively, you can use a baking dish big enough to hold the fish and bake the fish in a 350°F oven for about 25 minutes. Remove from the heat and let the fish cool in the liquid.

Remove the fish from the liquid and put on a work surface with the flatter side up. Peel back the skin on this side, leaving the head and tail intact, and cut neatly around the head and tail. Turn the fish over and peel the other side. Make a cut horizontally down the center of the salmon and gently separate the two pieces of fillet, then lift them off, being careful to keep them intact. Cut through the spine at the head and tail end and gently pull out the large bone. Pull out any bones that get left behind. Neatly replace the two pieces of fillet onto the lower fillet. Slice the cucumber into disks and then cut each one in half. Use these to decorate the salmon and hide the joins. Serve with lemon and mayonnaise.

Serves 8–10

Nigiri sushi

1 1/3 cups sushi rice
1/4 cup rice vinegar
2 teaspoons superfine sugar
2 (3 1/2-oz.) pieces of sashimi-grade
   tuna, cut into 8 rectangles
   measuring 2 x 1 1/4 x 1/4 inches
wasabi paste
Japanese soy sauce, for serving
pickled ginger, for serving

Fish substitution
   halibut, trout, salmon

Wash the rice under cold running water. Put the rice into a saucepan with 1 cup cold water. Cover the pan and bring to a boil. Reduce the heat and simmer for 10 minutes.

Meanwhile, mix 2 tablespoons of the vinegar, the sugar, and 1 teaspoon salt. When the rice is cooked, remove from the heat and let it cool, covered, for 10 minutes. Transfer the rice to a bowl. Add the vinegar mixture, bit by bit, turning and folding the rice in the bowl using a wooden spoon or spatula. Continue to fold until the rice is cool. Cover the pan with a damp towel and set aside—do not refrigerate.

When you are ready to form the sushi, mix the remaining vinegar with 1/4 cup water in a small bowl. Use the vinegar water to keep the rice from sticking to your fingers. Using 1 tablespoon of rice, put the rice in the palm of one hand and use the fingers of the other hand to form it into an oval shape. You should end up with sixteen ovals. Hold each oval in your hand and, using a finger, spread a smear of wasabi paste in the middle. Top each with a piece of fish, molding the fish onto the rice. Serve with soy sauce, extra wasabi, and pickled ginger.

Serves 4

Lobster thermidor

1 cooked lobster
6 tablespoons butter
4 scallions, finely chopped
1½ tablespoons all-purpose flour
½ teaspoon mustard powder
2 tablespoons white wine or sherry
1 cup milk
¼ cup cream
1 tablespoon chopped parsley
½ cup grated Gruyère cheese
lemon wedges, for serving

Using a sharp knife, cut the lobster in half lengthwise through the shell. Lift the meat from the tail and body. Remove the cream-colored vein and soft body matter and discard. Cut the meat into ¾-inch pieces, cover, and refrigerate. Wash the head and shell halves, then drain and pat dry.

Heat 4 tablespoons of the butter in a frying pan, add the scallions, and stir for 2 minutes. Stir in the flour and mustard and cook for 1 minute or until pale and foaming. Remove from the heat and gradually stir in the wine and milk. Return to the heat and stir constantly until the mixture boils and thickens. Reduce the heat and simmer for 1 minute. Stir in the cream, parsley, and lobster meat, then season with salt and pepper. Stir over low heat until the lobster is heated through.

Spoon the mixture into the lobster shells, sprinkle with cheese, and dot with the remaining butter. Place under a hot broiler and cook for 2 minutes or until lightly browned. Serve with salad and some lemon wedges.

Serves 2

Futomaki sushi

4 dried shiitake mushrooms
1 cup sushi rice
1 tablespoon rice vinegar
2 tablespoons plus two generous
    pinches superfine sugar
1 tablespoon mirin
½ small carrot, cut in half
1 large egg
1 teaspoon sake
1 teaspoon vegetable oil
2 sheets of toasted nori seaweed,
    each measuring 8 x 7 inches
2 sticks crabmeat, 1½ oz. each, cut
    into strips
1 oz. pickled daikon, cut into strips
1 oz. cucumber, cut into strips
Japanese soy sauce, for serving
wasabi paste, for serving
pickled ginger, for serving

Place the mushrooms in a small saucepan and cover with 1 1/4 cups boiling water. Place a saucer on top of the mushrooms to submerge them in the liquid, then leave to soak for 30 minutes.

Rinse the rice under cold running water. Put the rice in a saucepan and cover with a scant 1 cup cold water. Cover the pan and bring the water to a boil. Reduce the heat and simmer for 10 minutes.

While the rice is cooking, mix together the vinegar, a pinch of the sugar, and a generous pinch of salt. When the rice is cooked, remove the pan from the heat and let it stand, covered, for 10 minutes.

Transfer the rice to a bowl. Add the vinegar mixture, bit by bit, turning and folding the rice in the bowl using a wooden spoon or spatula. Continue to fold until the rice is cool. Cover the pan with a damp towel and set aside, but do not refrigerate.

Add the 2 tablespoons of sugar and the mirin to the mushrooms and stir. Add the carrots and bring the mixture to a simmer. Cook for 10 minutes, then drain. Discard the mushroom stalks and thinly slice the caps. Cut the carrot pieces into thin strips.

To make the omelette, gently mix together the egg, sake, the remaining pinch of sugar, and a pinch of salt. Heat the oil in a small frying pan. Add the egg mixture and cook until firm around the edges but still slightly soft in the middle. Roll the omelette and then tip it out of the pan and onto a bamboo mat. Roll the omelette in the mat and allow to cool, then slice into strips.

Place a sheet of nori on the mat, shiny-side down. Add half of the cooked rice, leaving a 3/4-inch gap at the edge furthest from you. Lay half of the filling ingredients on the rice in the following order: mushrooms, omelette, crabmeat, daikon, carrot, cucumber. Starting with the end nearest to you, tightly roll the mat and the nori. Repeat this process with the other piece of seaweed and remaining ingredients.

Using a sharp knife, cut each roll into six slices. After cutting each slice, rinse the knife under cold running water to prevent sticking. Transfer to a serving plate and serve with soy sauce, wasabi, and pickled ginger.

Serves 4

Cantonese-style steamed fish

2 lb. whole carp or barramundi, gutted through the gills, head and tail intact
2 tablespoons Chinese rice wine
1 ½ tablespoons soy sauce
1 teaspoon roasted sesame oil
4 tablespoons finely chopped fresh ginger
2 tablespoons vegetable oil
¼ cup finely shredded scallion

fish substitution
 sea bass

Put the fish in a large, nonmetallic bowl. Add the rice wine, soy sauce, sesame oil, and 1 tablespoon of the ginger and toss lightly to coat. Cover with plastic wrap and marinate in the fridge for 10 minutes.

Arrange the fish on a heatproof plate and put it in a steamer. Steam over simmering water in a covered wok for 5–8 minutes or until the flesh feels flaky when the skin is pressed firmly. Remove from the steamer.

Heat a wok over high heat. Add the vegetable oil and heat until smoking hot. Sprinkle the steamed fish with the scallion, the remaining ginger, and ¼ teaspoon freshly ground black pepper, then slowly pour the hot oil over the fish. This will cause the skin to crisp and the garnish to cook. Serve with rice and vegetables.

Serves 6

Basics

Buying and storing seafood

Crabs

Buy live crabs from a reputable source, as they are highly perishable. Look for lively crabs that feel heavy for their size. Crabs with worn barnacles and feet will not have just molted, and will have more meat. Mud crabs should be tied up until after they have been killed. Never buy a dead, uncooked crab. Store live crabs covered with a damp cloth in a closed container in the coldest part of the fridge for one to two days. To freeze, wrap in foil, put in an airtight bag, and freeze for up to three months.

Cooked crabs are also perishable, so buy with care. Make sure they smell fresh and are undamaged and their legs and feet are drawn into the body (if they were dead when cooked, their legs will be looser). Crabmeat is also available frozen, canned, and in vacuum-sealed plastic bags.

Crayfish

Live crayfish should feel heavy and still be fairly lively. If they have not been purged (had their guts cleaned out) before sale, crayfish need to have their guts removed before eating. Cooked crayfish should have their tails curled tightly against their bodies and smell sweet and look fresh. Never buy dead, uncooked crayfish.

Store live crayfish covered with a damp cloth in the salad compartment of the fridge for one to two days. To freeze, wrap the crayfish in foil, place in an airtight freezer bag, and freeze for up to three months.

Fish fillets/cutlets

Fillets or cutlets should look moist and have no signs of discoloration. The fish on display should not be sitting in liquid. Fresh fish fillets should not look dried at the edges.

Fish fillets and cutlets can be kept for one to two days in a covered container in the coldest part of the fridge. They can also be frozen in airtight bags for up to three months.

Lobsters

When buying a live lobster, make sure it is lively and has its tail tucked under its body. The shell should be hard—a soft shell indicates it has just molted and is not in peak condition. The shell should have no holes and the lobster should have all its limbs. When picking up a lobster, first make sure its claws are taped together, then pick it up just behind the head using your finger and thumb. Don't grasp it around its middle, as it might close up on you suddenly.

Store live lobsters covered with a damp cloth in the salad compartment of the fridge for one to two days.

To freeze, wrap the lobster in foil, place in an airtight freezer bag, and freeze for up to three months.

Don't buy dead, uncooked lobster, as there is no way of telling what condition it is in and the meat deteriorates quickly. Lobster can also be bought precooked—it should smell sweet and look fresh.

Mussels

Always buy mussels from a reputable source. Mussels are farmed extensively and these are safer to eat than wild ones, as mussels are filter-feeders and many harbor toxins. Fresh mussels must be bought live, as any that are dead may be toxic. The shells should be uncracked and closed, or should close when tapped on a countertop.

Store live mussels covered with a damp cloth in the salad compartment of the fridge for one to two days.

Octopus and squid

The flesh should be firm and resilient and spring back when touched. The head, tentacles, and body should be intact and not loose.

Fresh octopus and squid will last for one to two days in the fridge and for about three months in the freezer.

Oysters

Ideally, an oyster should be bought live, with the shell closed; it should be heavy and full of water. If buying an open oyster, prick the cilla (little hairs around the edge of the flesh): it should retract if the oyster is alive. Look for plump, glossy oysters that smell fresh. Unopened oysters can be kept in the fridge for up to a week. If opened, store in their liquid and eat within twenty-four hours. Do not freeze.

Shrimp

When buying raw shrimp, avoid limp and soft ones that smell of ammonia or have any black spots or juices around the shells and heads. Choose fully intact, firm, and crisp shrimp with bright shells and a fresh sea scent. Most seafood stores also sell precooked shrimp, which makes the preparation much easier.

Raw shrimp will keep for one to two days in a covered container in the coldest part of the fridge. To freeze, place in a plastic container and cover with water—this forms a large ice block, which insulates the shrimp and prevents freezer burn. Freeze for up to three months. When needed, thaw in the refrigerator overnight.

Scallops

Scallop flesh should be pale beige to light pink, moist, and glossy, with a fresh sea smell. The orange or pinkish red roe is also edible. Scallops are sold either still enclosed in their shells or removed from the shell (shucked). Because they deteriorate rapidly once out of the water, they are usually sold shucked and should be refrigerated quickly and used within one day. They can also be bought frozen.

Slipper lobsters
Slipper lobsters should have no discoloration or blackness, particularly at the joints. Bodies and claws should be fully intact. Bodies should be free of water or liquid and should be heavy in relation to their size.

When buying live slipper lobsters, they should be active and moving freely. Pincers and claws should be intact, not broken or loose. Store them covered with a damp cloth in the salad compartment of the fridge for one to two days. To freeze, wrap in foil, place in an airtight freezer bag, and freeze for up to three months.

Whole fish
Fish should be considered seasonal to really get the most out of them, as supplies will vary according to spawning seasons and fishing patterns. It is wise to buy the best fish that day, whatever it is, rather than an inferior fish just to fit a particular recipe.

Choose fish that have clear, bright, and bulging eyes and avoid fish that have dull, sunken, cloudy eyes.

The skin and flesh should have a lustrous appearance and feel firm. If a fish can easily be bent so its mouth can kiss its tail, it is probably past its prime. Fish with scales should have a good, even coverage; avoid those that look patchy. Gills should be bright (from bright to dark red, depending on species). Some fish, such as salmon and trout, are covered in a clear slime (old slime is opaque). Oily fish deteriorate faster than white fish, so be particularly vigilant when buying them.

Whole fish are best stored after they have been scaled and gutted (see page 391). Store in a covered container in the coldest part of the fridge for two to three days.

Preparing seafood

Butterflying sardines
Cut the head from the sardine, split open the belly with a sharp knife, and remove the insides. Open out the sardine and place, skin-side up, on a chopping board. Press lightly yet firmly to open out. Turn over and pull out the backbone. Cut off at the tail end of the bones. Wash in salted water and dry on paper towels.

Cleaning clams
Wash the clams in several changes of cold water, leaving them for a few

minutes each time to remove any grit. Scrub the clams well. Drain well. Discard any broken clams or open ones that don't close when tapped on the countertop.

Cleaning mussels
Only use closed mussels or mussels that close when tapped. Scrub the mussels with a stiff brush and pull out the hairy beards. Discard any broken mussels or open ones that don't close when tapped. Rinse well under cold running water.

Cleaning squid
To clean squid, gently pull the tentacles away from the tube—the intestines should come away at the same time. Remove the intestines from the tentacles by cutting under the eyes, then remove the beak by using your fingers to push up the center. Pull away the soft bone. Rub the tubes under cold running water and the skin should come away easily. Wash the tubes and tentacles and drain well. The flaps can also be used. Use the body, flap, and tentacles whole, or cut the body into rings.

Cutting round fish cutlets
Round fish (e.g., salmon, trout, and bream) have a round body and eyes on either side of the head. Scale and gut your fish (see page 391). Use a

large knife or, for a large fish, a cleaver to slice cutlets. A cutlet (sometimes called a steak) is a thick slice through the body of the fish. Hold the fish firmly and cut through. Separate the whole fish into cutlets. If not using immediately, wrap individually and freeze.

Filleting flat fish
Flat fish (e.g., Dover sole) can yield four fillets, two from each side. Scale and gut your fish (see page 391). With a filleting knife, lay the fish dark skin-side up. Cut behind the head, then down the center of the spine. Cut around the edge of each fillet and lift off, using the knife to cut between the fillet and the bone. Turn the fish over and remove the other two fillets in the same way.

Filleting round fish
Round fish (e.g., salmon, trout, and bream) yield two fillets, one from each side of the fish. Scale and gut your fish (see page 391). With a filleting knife, cut through the backbone and down the side of the head while using a sawing motion. To lift the fillet, start at the head end and run your knife blade between the flesh and the bones, keeping the knife close to the bone, until you reach the tail end. Turn the fish over and remove the other fillet in the same way.

Peeling and deveining shrimp
Using your fingers, pull the head away from the body, then pull off the legs and peel the shell away from the body. If the shrimp are to be served whole, they generally look better with the tails intact; otherwise they can be removed. Try to remove even the tiniest bits of shell so you don't crunch on them when eating. To remove the intestinal vein from shrimp, start at the head end and use a skewer or a small, finely pointed knife to remove the dark vein.

Preparing crabs
If the crabs are live, freeze them for an hour to immobilize them. Plunge them into boiling water for two minutes, then drain. Wash well with a stiff brush, then pat dry. Pull the apron back from underneath the crab and separate the shells. Remove the feathery gills and intestines. Twist off the claws. Using a cleaver or large knife, cut the crabs in half. Crack the claws using crab crackers or the back of a heavy knife.

Preparing octopus
Using a small knife, carefully cut between the head and tentacles of the octopus, just below the eyes. Grasp the body of the octopus and push the beak out and up through the center of the tentacles with your finger. Cut the eyes from the head of the octopus by slicing off a small round with a small, sharp knife. Discard the eye section. To clean the octopus, carefully slit through one side, avoiding the ink sac, and scrape out any gut from inside. When you have slit the head open, rinse under running water to remove any remaining gut.

Preparing lobster, cooked
Grasp the head and body with two hands and twist them firmly in opposite directions to release the tail. With kitchen scissors, cut down both sides of the shell on the underside, placing the scissors between the flesh and soft shell. Peel back the soft undershell to reveal the flesh. Gently pull out the flesh in one piece. Scrape the meat out of the claws with a lobster pick. Gently pull out the vein, starting at the head, or remove when cutting the lobster into medallions or pieces.

Preparing lobster, live
Lobster bought live has the best flavor. The most humane way to kill lobster and other crustaceans is to put them in the freezer for an hour, then plunge in boiling water.

Cut into the membrane on the underside of the lobster, where the head and body join, to loosen. Twist or cut off to remove the tail. Cut down both sides of the shell on the underside, between the flesh and soft undershell, using a pair of scissors. Peel back the soft undershell. Gently pull out the flesh in one piece. Pull out the vein from the back with your fingers, or when cutting.

Preparing scallops

If you are using scallops still enclosed in their shells, start by scrubbing clean the shells. For easy shucking, put under a broiler for a minute to warm. Hold the scallop in a towel and, with a sharp knife, carefully pry open the shell. Lift off the top shell. Loosen the scallop from the shell.

With a small, sharp knife, carefully slice off and discard any vein, membrane, or hard, white muscle from each scallop. The pinky red roe is edible but may be removed.

Scaling and gutting fish

Fish need to be gutted fairly quickly, as their digestive juices can break down and start to decompose their flesh. If possible, scale your fish outdoors, in a plastic bag or in the sink. Hold the fish firmly at the tail. Lifting it slightly, scrape against the direction of the scales with a fish scaler or sharp knife. Rinse well. Use a sharp knife to slit the belly, then remove the gut. Rinse under cold water, then pat dry with paper towels.

Shucking oysters

Wrap a towel around the unshucked oyster. Work an oyster shucker into the oyster and twist to break the hinge. Remove the top shell and slip the shucker between the oyster and the shell to release. Rinse both to remove grit. Replace the oyster.

Skinning a fish fillet

Depending on the recipe, you may or may not need to skin your fish. If the fish will be covered with a sauce, it will be easier to eat the fish with its skin removed. Remove the skin before cooking, or if cooking a whole fish, carefully peel it off after cooking. To skin a fillet, lay the fillet skin-side down on a board, with its tail toward you. Make a small cut through the flesh to the skin. Put the knife blade through the cut against the skin and slide or push the blade away from you. Hold the skin firmly. Continue sliding the blade up to the head. You may need to move the blade from side to side as the fillet gets thicker.

Skinning Dover sole

Dover sole can have their skins removed whole. To do this, make a small cut at the tail end and loosen a piece of skin, then hold the fish down with one hand and the skin in the other and firmly pull it toward the head—it should peel off.

Cooking and serving seafood

Serving whole fish
Run a spoon or knife down the center of the fish, then pull the fish from the bone. Lift out all the bones and cut off near the tail. Serve the fish in sections.

Testing fish for doneness
Most fish is cooked when it loses its translucent appearance and turns opaque. When tested with a fork, the flesh starts to flake and separate from the bone. Some fish, such as tuna and Atlantic salmon, are best served while still rare in the center. Don't overcook fish; take it off the heat as soon as it is "just done"—the internal heat will finish the cooking process.

Testing mollusks for doneness
Mollusks can be cooked briefly or eaten raw. The shells can be pried open—you may need to cut the muscle, or they can be steamed open.

Testing shrimp for doneness
When shrimp are cooked, they should have turned pink and be curled.

Testing seafood for doneness
Most seafood is cooked when it loses its translucent appearance and turns opaque. Don't overcook seafood or it will be dry, tough, and rubbery.

Basic recipes

Court bouillon
Pour 8 cups dry white wine, ¼ cup white wine vinegar, and 10 cups water into a large saucepan. Stud 2 onions with 5 cloves each and add to the pan along with 4 chopped carrots, 1 quartered lemon, 2 bay leaves, 4 sprigs of parsley, and 1 teaspoon black peppercorns. Bring to a boil, reduce the heat, and simmer for 30–35 minutes. Remove the bay leaves. Makes 15 cups.

Fish stock
Put 4 lb. 8 oz. chopped, clean fish trimmings, 1 roughly chopped celery stalk (including the leaves), 1 chopped onion, 1 unpeeled chopped carrot, 1 sliced leek, 1 bouquet garni, 12 black peppercorns, and 8 cups water in a large saucepan. Bring slowly to a boil and carefully skim off any froth that forms on the surface, using a sieve or ladle. Reduce the heat to low and simmer very gently for 20 minutes. Skim the froth from the surface regularly. Ladle the stock into a sieve, lined with damp muslin, sitting over a bowl. To keep the stock clear, do not press the solids, but simply allow the stock to strain undisturbed. Cool, then refrigerate for up to a week, or freeze. Makes 7 cups.

Alternative names

anchovies *smig*
Atlantic salmon *salmon trout*
bonito *horse mackerel*
bream *porgy, silver or black bream*
coley *coalfish, saithe*
crab, blue *Atlantic blue crab, soft-shelled crab*
dabs *dab sole, flounder, garve, sand dab*
Dover sole *common sole, sole*
Dublin bay prawn *Langoustine, Norway lobster, scampi*
eel *European eel*
European carp *mirror, calico carp*
garfish *sea garfish, garpike, sea eel, needlefish*
grouper *hapuka, bass grouper*
John Dory *St. Peter's fish, kuparu*
kingfish *yellowtail, southern yellowtail, southern yellowfish*
lemon sole *lemon dab, lemon fish*
ling *rock ling*
mahimahi *dolphinfish, dorado*
monkfish *anglerfish, stargazer*
mullet, red *goatfish, barbounia, rouget*
mullet, sea *gray mullet*
orange roughy *red roughy, sea perch, deep-sea perch*
parrotfish *tuskfish*
perch, ocean *coral perch*
pike *short fin pike, sea pike*
pilchards *adult sardines*
Pollack *green fish, lythe*

redfish *nannygai, red snapper*
sardine *bluebait pilchards (adult)*
scorpion fish *red rock cod*
shark *flake*
skate *ray*
snapper *cockney bream, red bream*
sole *see Dover sole*
squid *calamari*
trevally *skippy, jack*
trout, coral *leopard, blue spot trout*
trout, rainbow *river trout, steelhead trout*
tuna, bluefin *southern bluefin*
warehou, blue *snotty-nose trevalla, black travalla, snotgall trevally*
whiting, sand *silver whiting*

Index

Index

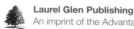

Laurel Glen Publishing
An imprint of the Advantage Publishers Group
5880 Oberlin Drive, San Diego, CA 92121-4794
www.laurelglenbooks.com

All notations of errors or omissions should be addressed to Laurel Glen Publishing, Editorial Department, at the above address. All other correspondence (author inquiries, permissions, and rights) concerning the content of this book should be addressed to Murdoch Books® a division of Murdoch Magazines Pty Ltd, Pier 8/9, 23 Hickson Road, Millers Point NSW 2000, Australia.

NOTE: Those who might be at risk from the effects of salmonella poisoning (the elderly, pregnant women, young children, and those with a compromised immune system) should consult their physician before trying recipes made with raw eggs.

ISBN 1-59223-275-2
Library of Congress Cataloging-in-Publication Data available upon request.

Printed by Tien Wah Press, Singapore
1 2 3 4 5   08 07 06 05 04

Editor: Zoë Harpham
Editorial Director: Diana Hill
Designer: Michelle Cutler
Creative Director: Marylouise Brammer
Photographers: Jared Fowler, Ian Hofstetter
Stylists: Katy Holder, Cherise Koch
Food Preparation: Michelle Earl, Jo Glynn
Production: Monika Paratore
Recipes developed by the Murdoch Books Test Kitchen
Chief Executive: Juliet Rogers
Publisher: Kay Scarlett

You may find cooking times vary depending on the oven you are using. For convection ovens, as a general rule, set the oven temperature 40°F lower than indicated in the recipe.
We have used large eggs in all recipes.

The publisher thanks Steve Costi Seafoods for their assistance in the photography for this book.